AN
ANOINTED
Mess

AN ANOINTED

Discovering the Daily
Adventure of Grace

KAREN PENNINGTON

REDEMPTION
PRESS

Published by Redemption Press, PO Box 427, Enumclaw, WA 98022.

Toll-Free (844) 2REDEEM (273-3336)

Redemption Press is honored to present this title in partnership with the author. The views expressed or implied in this work are those of the author. Redemption Press provides our imprint seal representing design excellence, creative content, and high quality production.

ISBN 13: 978-1-64645-478-5 (Paperback)
978-1-64645-479-2 (ePub)
978-1-64645-480-8 (Mobi)

Library of Congress Catalog Card Number: 2021906591

In the following pages, I share real stories about actual events that happened throughout my life. In order to guard the privacy of those involved, I have changed all names in my personal stories other than those of myself, my family, my pastor, and my dog.

Karen

CONTENTS

OUR SHARED JOURNEY
The Stories We Tell Together

Through the gospel Gentiles are heirs together with Israel, members together of one body, and sharers together in the promise in Christ Jesus.
Ephesians 3:6

THE BIBLE IS THE WORLD'S LARGEST ANTHOLOGY OF seriously messed up people. Some of their dysfunctions stick out more notably. Judah unknowingly impregnated his daughter-in-law, mistaking her for a prostitute, and then he almost had her killed. Nebuchadnezzar spent a period wherein he literally thought and acted like a wild animal, grass-eating and all. Rachel sold sexual rights to her husband Jacob for the bargain price of a few pieces of fruit, and Jacob remarkably went along with it. Peter cut off the ear of a man who had never so much as approached him.

Then again, not all of the types of personal issues listed in the pages of Scripture would make the six o'clock news nowadays. Some appear more subtle, more "normal" if you will. Noah had a drinking problem. Leah lived in a loveless marriage. Eli dealt with a weight issue. Jesus himself could not seem to get his brothers to take him seriously. Then there were the countless money issues, the people who could barely—if at all—afford to feed their families.

I love that God's Word does not merely outline a bunch of spotless, picture-perfect personalities and lifestyles that I could never attain.

It is about people who struggled, just like me. Sometimes they struggled with sin. Sometimes, even with the purest of intentions, they suffered at the hands of a world they could not control.

Herein lies the true meaning of grace. God's blessings do not fly loftily above, around, or even despite our weaknesses and suffering. Grace reaches right through them. We generally desire for God to just take our pains and weaknesses away. More often, if we pay careful and faithful attention, the Lord transforms them to strengthen us and show us God's glory.

It makes no difference whether our struggles seem big or small, life-changing or mildly annoying. For some reason many of us tend to think of God as the Lord of the mountains and the valleys, the Great One who meets us at the extraordinary points of glory and despair. But the landscape of life is far richer than the peaks and lows, and the Lord is the architect of it all.

We easily forget that the Lord has an extraordinary ability to bring about the most amazing results from seemingly ordinary circumstances. It is not a matter of our seeking for God to enter our everyday lives. Our Daddy[1] never leaves us.

Our task is rather to recognize God's miraculous presence at work *within* our daily struggles. As we learn to receive and live by God's merciful power and plan, we become both witnesses to and bearers of heavenly grace. This grace reaches deep enough to cover every crevice of our souls and broad enough to sweep through every iota of our lives.

I write these words to you as a person who is very much a work in progress if you will. I am definitely not one of those women you see who always seems so well put together. There's always something out of place in my life, whether it be messy hair, an unironed shirt, a cluttered house, or a general state of minor panic that accompanies the many unorganized details in my brain. Someone once accurately pointed out to me that I always seem to be struggling with something in my life: finances, family, my weight—you get the picture.

---

1 Even Jesus called God Daddy. Mark 14:36, Romans 8:15, and Galatians 4:6 all refer to the Lord as "Abba," a Hebrew word that roughly translates to mean "Daddy."

However, I am also one of the happiest, most joyful people I know, and I would not trade my life with anyone on this planet. I do not agree with those self-help books that point to a promise of joy and fulfillment on the other side of the struggle. If this were the case, we could not find joy on this side of Heaven. Whose life is ever free of some sort of annoyance? I believe that God can grant any of us victory and peace right within the struggle, while at the same time constantly moving us forward in grace. I have yet to find the antidote to all of life's problems, but you know what? God still uses and blesses me, even with my messed-up hair and wrinkled shirt.

Praise the Lord, I am an anointed mess!

The following chapters reflect on some of the ways God's grace has reached in and through various issues within society, the Bible, and my own life. Together these different snapshots form a collage of human existence. Though the pictures show many flaws, they also reflect on a perfect empowerment and illumination that binds all things together for the good of all who love the Lord.

The perspectives from my own stories reflect my personal reality as experienced at different points of my journey. I thought it important to present the unpolished, raw voice of a person in process, rather than going back and redacting my perspective from years past.

The final anecdote in each chapter is yours. Along with the stories, I encourage you to read the listed Bible passages in full, and to use the questions as a guide to further self-discovery. You may choose to do so within a small group community or as part of your personal devotional time.

I hope and pray that as you read these you will discover the power of our story. I say "our story" because I believe that the chapters of our lives are so intimately connected with one another that we cannot truly know our own story outside of sharing and telling it together in community with others.

Consider yourself invited to march right up onto life's stage and claim your role within this great divine drama of grace. May it help you to discovery and begin to write your own book of faith within your heart!

CHAPTER 1

THE WHACK OF JUSTICE
Guiding Grace

"For I know the plans I have for you," declares the Lord, "plans to prosper you and not to harm you, plans to give you hope and a future."
Jeremiah 29:11

OUR STORY

I believe that the Lord has implanted within every human being a strong desire for justice. It comes to us as part of the package deal of our being made in God's image. We cannot in any way resemble God if we do not, to some degree, possess in our innermost core an intense yearning for what is good and right.

At its best, this sense, a most holy gift from God, can enable us to help maintain peace and restore order to the Lord's fallen creation. Acting as a spiritual compass, it can point us to the very heartbeat of the Holy One.

As is the case with most of God's originally perfect gifts, we humans somehow find a way to mess this one up almost immediately. Some might argue that the moment we leave the womb we begin to confuse what is right for what we want. The baby girl's endless cries in the middle of the night tend to have little to do with what her parents deserve, or even what she needs, and everything to do with what she desires that very minute.

Indeed, it seems that right from the start the great accuser[2] recruits soldiers by offering us this additive of self-centeredness to pollute our pure sense of justice thoroughly and completely. He has perfected the craft in this country, where so many seem to possess little to no understanding of the difference between what is right and what is my right. Thus begins the fighting: on the battlefields, in the courts, in the homes, and in every other place that human breath and being exist. Inevitably, our rights will infringe upon one another to the point where someone will always suffer injustice.

We have all played the game and struggled with the question of where to draw the lines. You have a right to smoke a cigarette in public, and I have a right to live in a smoke-free environment. You have the right to charge whatever rent you choose for the apartments you own, and I have a right to affordable housing. You have the right to speak and dress as you like, and I have the right to live in an environment free from vulgarity. You have the right to carry a gun everywhere, and I have a right to live without fear of being shot down. So which right is right?

The hardest question for me to answer comes with regard to our relationship with authority. The Bible clearly states that we should submit to earthly authorities insofar as they do not keep us from following God's greater will. So, what if we suspect that our earthly authorities (parents, employers, governments, church leaders, etc.) point us to those things that do not please God? When do we trust them, and at what point should we determine to take matters into our own hands?

The answer to this question cannot come in any pat reply, but rather through a journey into the heart of God. This journey involves the surrender of our every footstep to the one whose will we may not always understand.

MY STORY

I have always had a strong personal sense of justice, however skewed it may have been in my early childhood. For example, family

---

2 The name Satan comes from the Hebrew word meaning "the accuser."

members enjoy reminding me about my first act of "civil disobedience," which I carried out as a mere toddler.

The target was the only authority I knew then, my parents. At that time, my mother held to a fairly regular ritual of spanking me for those habits which I felt I had every right to do. The habits themselves carry no real importance. I cannot remember them myself. What I do remember even that far back is that my mother's hand on my backside hurt, and I did not like it one bit.

Even back then I liked to have my own say in things, so for Mommy to punish me in such a way without first asking my opinion upset me. My cries must have made it clear to her that I did not like the spankings, yet she continued the ritual as she felt the need to do so.

So, on that one fateful day, at the tender age of two, I decided to take matters into my own little hands.

The plan came after yet another spanking, when at last I could take it no more. Surely Grandma Hunter had not been this cruel to Mom. So I decided that the only way to open Mommy's eyes to the error of her ways was to teach her a lesson about the pain of her own spankings.

Since I could not quite reach high enough on my own, I began to look around the house for some sort of equalizer to help me administer this justice. Fortunately for me, Daddy was in the middle of doing some work on the bathroom. That left a nice, toddler-sized two-by-four plank of scrap wood lying around within my reach.

When Mommy went to check on the wash, I knew my chance had come. I grabbed the two-by-four and quietly snuck up behind her. As she bent down to put the washed clothes into the dryer, I whacked her on the behind with all of my might. It did not quite push her into the dryer, as I hoped, but I did get her attention. I reasoned that one small tap for this little girl was a giant whack for human justice.

When Mommy turned around and stood up with a confused, bewildered look on her face, I was ready for her. I dropped the two-by-four, put one hand on my hip, and pointed the other straight at her. Putting on my most serious face, I cried out "Now you know what it feels like."

I knew I needed to make this point, no matter what happened to me. I did not care if Mommy spanked me or took away my toys. But what she did was worse. After a few short moments of attempted composure, Mommy threw up her hands, put down her head, and just broke out laughing.

Needless to say, the spankings did not stop altogether, though I amused her enough to keep myself from punishment on that particular afternoon. Eventually I found a more effective means of preventing the unpleasant swats. I simply chose to obey.

GOD'S STORY

Through the prophet Jeremiah, God—Israel's heavenly parent—warned them over and over again about the coming consequences of their disobedience. Through the years God's disciplinary action increased in severity: from lost battles to a divided kingdom, to military occupation, until eventually a mass deportation and the obliteration of Judah's capital city, Jerusalem.

Given a deep history of God's provision and faithfulness, one might think that this occupation by a foreign army would have turned the eyes of the Israelites in Judah upon the Lord. This was not the case, at least not immediately. Like children, the Israelites' first reaction was to mope and whine. The second was to take matters into their own hands, wondering what they might do to defeat their oppressors, with or without God.

The history of the Old Testament proved that doing things on their own was never a good idea for God's people. It left them wandering, defeated, or divided for much longer than if they just would have repented and trusted God in the first place. Within the first few years of his reign, the disobedience of Israel's fourth king, Rehoboam, led to a complete schism in the nation, creating the northern kingdom of Israel and the southern kingdom of Judah.

A few hundred years later, the Kingdom of Assyria overtook the northern kingdom of Israel as a consequence of their continued reckless disregard for God's law. Judah did not heed the strong warning

God sent through the destruction of her sister nation. Over a hundred years later, the people of Judah still continued their adulterous and double-minded practices.

With the rising eastern kingdom of Babylon breathing down their necks, they had good reason to turn back to the Lord for help. Foreseeing their impending doom, the prophet Jeremiah continually cried out to the Israelites of Judah to repent and turn back to God before something worse happened. Still, they refused to change their ways. Rather than surrendering to the Lord, Judah responded by fighting their oppressors directly. Without God, they had no power to fight, and things only got worse.

Consequently, the Neo-Babylonian Empire of the Chaldeans overtook Judah and gradually forced the nation into submission. One king after another fell, until eventually the Chaldeans completely destroyed the capital city of Jerusalem and called for a mass deportation of the Israelites to Babylon. Finally, they stopped resisting their mortal enemies. Unfortunately, rather than turning their focus upward toward God, they focused inward in self-pity.

The people of Judah had ignored God and his prophets for hundreds of years, despite all the signs and warnings God sent. Then, when they received exactly what they deserved in the exile, they were ready to give up on God, once again confusing justice with getting what they wanted.

Fortunately, God had not given up on them, and neither had Jeremiah. Eventually, some of them started to pay attention to God's words through the prophet. Sometimes God needs to bring us to the point of utter despair before we are willing to listen to the truth that has been so obvious all along.

Through Jeremiah, God cried out to the people of Judah, saying "Hey there, I love you, and I know what I'm doing. This may seem like the end for you, but it is just the beginning. You may not understand this now, but some day you'll thank me for it. Just hang in there with me and trust me" (Jeremiah 29:11–13, Pennington Paraphrase).

In truth, our loving God does not punish people to enjoy the justice of their suffering, or even to vindicate God's way. The driving force behind all good discipline from either our earthly or heavenly parent is love, not anger or retribution. It helps us remember when we are going beyond healthy boundaries, and it seeks to keep us from worse consequences that an often-unloving world could inflict upon us.

As a child of God, I all too often revert back to my own self-centered, self-righteous form of justice. God is even more patient than my earthly mother, and together we are working on my growing in obedience.

As a toddler, I misunderstood the grace my mother practiced by addressing my poor behavior. As the parent, I now understand the meaning and value of proper discipline. My daughter Alethea (Ali) is so much like me. As I struggle to help her understand boundaries and consequences, I find I am becoming more in tune with the heart of my heavenly nurturer who always has my best life in mind.

Still, while engrossed in our own house renovation during Ali's toddler years, I was quite careful to keep the scrap lumber out of reach!

> *Lord,* You are an eternally just and gracious God. How often do I seek my own vindication above your will? How many times have I reacted in anger toward your loving chastisement, ignoring the value of your holy discipline? Forgive me, Lord. I now know that your chastisement is part of your heavenly nurture of us all. May I never forget.

YOUR STORY

Read and reflect upon Jeremiah 29:4–14. Then consider the following questions:

1. Did the Israelites from Judah have a right to be mad at God for allowing them to be taken into exile? Why or why not?

2. Was it wise for the Israelites from Judah to try dealing with the Chaldeans on their own? Why or why not?

3. Is there a connection between obeying God and obeying human authorities? What is it?

4. Has there ever been a time when your children or others under your authority misunderstood discipline that you administered for their good? Has there ever been a time when you misunderstood the disciplinary actions that God, your parents, or other authorities have shown you? Has there been a time when you thought "They're out to get me," when they were actually trying to help you out?

5. Have you ever been caught and punished for knowingly breaking a rule? When that happens, does it upset you more that you are caught or that you have done something wrong?

6. Are you currently facing a bad situation as a consequence of your own sin or disobedience? How are you handling it? Are you taking matters into your own hands, or are you actively seeking and trusting God to help you through it?

CHAPTER 2

FACING THE GIANT
Defiant Grace

*Be strong and courageous. . . . for the Lord your God will be with you
wherever you go.*
Joshua 1:9

OUR STORY

In the early 1980s, First Lady Nancy Reagan led a historic anti-drug campaign that targeted school children. As an antidote to the peer pressure and temptation many felt to use or even sell illegal drugs, Mrs. Reagan's campaign offered this simple three-word phrase: Just Say No.

This powerful mini-sentence quickly became a catchphrase for a great deal of American life. Just Say No, so simple yet so broad, applied to countless other circumstances within an overindulgent culture. To those who tried not to eat too much . . . just say no. To those whom co-workers pushed around with unfair requests . . . just say no. To those who felt pressured to participate in any sort of illegal, immoral, or unhealthy activity . . . just say no.

On paper and coming out of people's mouths, this sounded like excellent advice. But when the rubber hit the road, many realized that the method turned out quite a lot trickier than the slogan promised.

When applied to other situations, the wording seems down-right silly. If a car broke down and the owner asked how to get it running, would a mechanic respond by saying *"just* fix it"? Could a dietician with whom an overweight person consults adequately save time on the full consultation by repeating only three words of advice, *"just* lose weight"? Could we all accurately and efficiently respond to world hunger by telling the starving people that they should *"just* go eat"?

Critics of the phrase might note that the word "just" both under-estimates and oversimplifies the extreme difficulty many people have with saying no, especially in the face of their personal circumstances. Another *just* slogan, "just do it," seems more compelling in a "yes" society that stresses going for it, letting go of inhibitions, or giving in to the temptation. Most advertising thrives on these thoughts.

In many people's minds, Just Say No sometimes translates to mean *"just* do the impossible." This seems even beyond impossible for those who seek to do God's will. The Bible clearly and consistently emphasizes the virtues of obedience and submission, along with a command to keep the peace when possible. On the surface, defiance and refusal appear diabolically opposed to these values.

However, Christians have a responsibility to dig beneath life's façade in search of God's deeper truth. In reality, God calls us out to stand against evil and injustice. Indeed, we cannot live in obedience and submission to God without also actively resisting the forces that oppose the Lord's way.

This begs the question: how does a person say no to such things when virtually all of life's circumstances compel that person to say yes? Even more so, once the words fly out of a brave soul's mouth, how might that person find the courage to stand by them when faced with a world that pulls in the exact opposite direction?

It would help to have some magic key or special one-size-fits-all formula for defiance of evil and vice. Truthfully, different people get to that point in different ways, down their own paths. Sometimes it really is as simple as just saying no. Sometimes it takes years, far more words, and one or more direct interventions from God to bring about this revolution against the wrong. Regrettably, many never get there.

One thing is for sure. When we get to the point of sacred defiance, of standing up to anything that holds us back or drags us down, that little two letter word "No" can *just* unlock amazing power within our lives and our world.

MY STORY

At the record height of twelve feet seven inches (or so it seemed), Erica Rollins towered over everyone else in the schoolyard. The fact that she stood as much as a head or more over the rest of us, combined with her even bigger mouth, yielded a recipe of mass intimidation. She even scared the sixth graders.

Her entourage of friends and supporters added to the threat. They seemed to travel everywhere with her, even to the bathroom. Had we any doubt of her ability to hurt us, we knew that the other members of the Rollins posse would cover her back, defeating any challengers by sheer numbers. It was one thing to face off against the quarterback, but to challenge an entire football team without expecting to be tackled would prove sheer madness.

Erica claimed ownership rights to anything in sight, freely taking whatever she wanted from others in class. Of course, she would always do so at times when our teacher had his back turned or stepped out of the room, or when we had a substitute. I think the substitute teachers were scared of her too. No one dared tell on her. No one dared challenge her by asking for their things back. Most of us valued our lives more than we valued our crayons.

When I thought about it, I realized no one in class had ever actually seen her beat anyone up. Kids just assumed that she would fight them when she did not get what she wanted, and that when she fought them, she would win. She truly reminded me of those pirates I saw in the movies whom people would fear based on their reputations—all bark and no bite. Still, I felt rather unwilling to find out just how hard she could bite when provoked, so I kept my distance.

For the most part, Erica left me alone as well. Perhaps my relative largeness kept her from tempting fate. Maybe she just realized that I did not fear her quite as much as the others. Perhaps my desk's position in the far corner of the room, at the end of the last row, kept her from bothering to make the trip over.

One day she decided to make the trip anyhow, her eyes set on some valuable booty. She had unfortunately noticed my recent acquisition of a liquid glue stick, the first of its kind in our class. She waited until I needed to step away from my desk for a moment. Then, as I watched from across the room, she just sauntered over, reached her hand inside my desk, took the glue stick, and walked away like nothing happened.

Most of the kids ignored this, her ritual offense. It infuriated me. I already held a special contempt for other children who tried to steal from me. Add to this the fact that the liquid glue stick came as part of a special gift from my mother, which really meant something to a child in a large family that lived on a very modest income. I simply could not allow anyone to mess with that.

Though unsure of what she might do as a consequence, I decided to take action. Death could not keep me from my glue stick. Without saying anything, I walked right up to her, grabbed the glue stick out of her hand even while she used it, and walked back to my seat.

This caught the eye of most everyone in class. Even those who did not originally see what had happened (including our teacher) took notice as Erica yelled at me across the room. "Girl, what do you think you're doing?"

All heads snapped in our direction in stunned silence, wondering what I would say. I didn't care. I liked attention. As the youngest child in my family, I practically lived for attention.

"This is mine," I yelled back.

Taken aback, she struggled to maintain her bully composure. "So? I was using it."

"You don't just take people's stuff without asking. It's rude," I responded heatedly. What made her think she could just walk all over people? This time she had stepped too far. Of course, had I thought these things out ahead of time, good sense may have led me to step back.

However, in this case, my impulsiveness served me well. The Rollins posse seemed to dissipate into thin air, like a retreating cavalry that had not prepared for battle. With the teacher now watching, Erica faced the dilemma of how to gain the upper hand, while at the same time avoiding punishment. She couldn't do it. Instead, she reverted to her own version of half-hearted manners.

"Well, fine then. Can I use your glue stick?"

"No way."

"Why not?"

"I would have let you use it if you asked me in the first place. Since you just stole it without asking, you can't have it at all now."

Erica just stood there for a moment, dumfounded. Then, to everyone's surprise, she simply said "Okay, be like that then," and went about her business. Suddenly she did not seem so tall to us anymore.

Some of my classmates must have felt at first that I had sealed my doom by denying our classroom giant her spoils. Had I declared war on Goliath, or perhaps on the entire enemy army?

On the contrary, things got better. I think she sort of respected me for speaking my mind. She also started to be a little nicer to everyone else. I accidentally did a small thing, mostly out of anger, that led to a much better life for many of us throughout elementary school. In the end, the feared giant eventually even became a friend.

GOD'S STORY

The people of Judah had a bigger enemy to fear than an overgrown kid. The Chaldean King Nebuchadnezzar gave them every reason to toe the line, to do everything he said. When Judah's King Jehoiakim decided to rebel (which by the way, went against God's own orders), Nebuchadnezzar completely destroyed its capital city, Jerusalem. With Jerusalem sacked, he ordered a mass deportation of the people of Judah to his own capital city of Babylon.

In efforts to crush any memory or hope of return to their Jerusalem life, King Neb called up all the best and brightest young men of Judah into his own court. Knowing that these would inevitably serve as the cultural leaders of their people, he began a systematic enculturation, a sophisticated brainwashing campaign that would inevitably trickle down to the commoners.

The young men learned Babylonian culture and language from the best teachers. They wore the finest Babylonian clothes. They comingled with the most beautiful Babylonian women. They sat in direct service to the Babylonian King, eating the best foods and drinking the finest wine from Nebuchadnezzar's own table. Then they received lofty titles and lucrative positions as governors and leaders throughout the Babylonian Empire.

The message seemed clear. Having seen both the devastating arm of the king's wrath and the decadent arm of his favor, most young Hebrews of Judah must have felt compelled to stay on his good side. Many surely chose to forget the brokenness of Jerusalem, along with all of that for which it stood. They surely chose to live fully in this glorious new world of beauty, strength, and luxury, and to advise their people to do the same.

The shrewd ruler even changed the young men's names. This may not seem like much to us nowadays, in a culture of nicknames, pseudonyms, and stage names. Back then it meant everything. In both the Old and New Testaments, when God changed a person's name, God simultaneously redefined that person's identity, rerouting their entire destiny.

In his attempt at playing God, King Nebuchadnezzar tried to do the same. For three men in particular, it did not work. Regardless of their new legal titles, these three forgot neither who they were nor *whose* they were.

They came to Babylon with the Hebrew names Hananiah (meaning "the Lord is gracious"), Mishael ("who is what God is?"), and Azariah ("the Lord has helped me"). The Chaldeans called them Shadrach, Meshach, and Abednego, names that in contrast honored three of that pagan culture's false gods.

To seal the deal, Nebuchadnezzar erected a golden statue in his own honor that stood about ninety feet high and ninety feet wide. He ordered all men in his service to bow down and worship the idol as a sign of their assimilation and allegiance to him as their god. To bow down would mean acceptance and prosperity. To remain standing would mean death by fire. You can imagine how few people in the crowd stayed on their feet—three to be exact.

So here stood the three friends, in the crowd of at least hundreds, maybe thousands. Having lost their homes, their families, and most of their earthly possessions, they knew what horrors this king's wrath could bring. Having received high honors and leadership positions in Babylon, along with the availability of every possible human luxury, they had a lot to lose. Here they stood, in the shadow of an idol as tall as an eight-story building, with a choice to make.

Such a small distance lay between their mounting prosperity and the impending doom. They only needed to bend their knees. They did not actually need to worship the statue, or even say words at all. They could have just bowed down, closed their eyes, and prayed to the real God. No one on earth would have known the difference. This reasoning surely compelled other sincere believers to bend down.

And yet they stood.

What a great opportunity for their enemies! A group of the natives felt pretty slighted at the fact that the king had chosen to hand over some of the choice ruling positions to the despised foreigners, rather than themselves. They took this opportunity to point the three out to the king, hoping to nab their jobs once the king had them executed.

Nebuchadnezzar threw a fit. Had these been men he detested, or whom he did not know so well, he may have simply and calmly disposed of them without a second thought. But Nebuchadnezzar seemed to like these guys. However, he could allow no sympathy for their strong act of civil disobedience that threatened to undermine his authority.

After yelling at them a little, the typically harsh ruler gave the three friends a second chance, even noting that he would wait until they were ready. He almost nicely warned them that he would have to throw them into the furnace, and that no god could possibly save them from the punishment.

Perhaps now, having heard the king's compelling plea and having had time to think about it, they would do the logical thing and bow down.

Nope. Instead, they blatantly shot him down. Delivering the Magna Carta of holy defiance, they said: "If we are thrown into the blazing furnace, the God we serve is able to deliver us from it, and he will deliver us from Your Majesty's hand. But even if he does not, we want you to know, Your Majesty, that we will not serve your gods or worship the image of gold you have set up" (Daniel 3:17–18).

They just said no.

At this point the gloves came off. No more mister nice king. "Then Nebuchadnezzar was furious with Shadrach, Meshach and Abednego, and his attitude toward them changed. He ordered the furnace heated seven times hotter than usual and commanded some of the strongest soldiers in his army to tie up Shadrach, Meshach, and Abednego and throw them into the blazing furnace. So these men, wearing their robes, trousers, turbans, and other clothes, were bound and thrown into the blazing furnace" (Daniel 3:19–21).

The flames burned so hot and high that they killed the king's men who stood with Shadrach, Meshach, and Abednego at the mouth of the furnace. They did not even have the chance to untie them and throw them in. Instead, the three fell in, ropes, clothes, and all.

Miraculously, the only things the fire burned off the three friends were the ropes binding them. (Or perhaps that fourth mysterious person who appeared in the furnace with them untied them.) They did not receive so much as a bruise from the fall, and the fire did not leave so much as the smell of smoke on their clothes.

Once again Nebuchadnezzar's countenance changed: from bewilderment at seeing the fourth man, to surprise at noticing the unharmed three, to praise and honor of their God, the one *true* God.

Hananiah, Mishael, and Azariah dared to stand up to one of the biggest bullies in all history. In response, God moved through them to change a possibly disastrous display into an encounter with the divine.

Upon reflection of my brush with the schoolyard bully, I realize that I would do well to apply that sort of defiance more when standing in the face of life's injustice and despair. That may mean allowing myself to get angrier about right things, stifling my anger about the wrong things, and praying for wisdom to know the difference.

It may be as simple as following that great phrase and daring to just say no. However difficult it may seem, it works.

> *Lord*, you are a God of justice, strength, and valor. Please forgive me for those times when I ought to have stood tall on your behalf, but I instead sat back in fear. Please open my eyes and heart, that I may see it when you call me to move forward and stand boldly in your name. I cannot stand on my own, but with your calling, and in your strength, I open my heart to your use, to advance your kingdom against the powers of the dark world. May I never forget that you are still on the throne, so I need not fear.

YOUR STORY

Read and reflect upon Daniel 2:39–4:3. Then consider the following questions:

1. What reasons compelled the other Israelites to bow to the statue when the three friends stood?

2. What was it about Nebuchadnezzar that you think seemed most intimidating, or fear-inspiring to these people?

3. What compelled the three friends to stand? Was there a difference between bowing as a subject of the king and bowing down to this statue?

4. What or who intimidates (or has intimidated) you in life? What is it about them that makes (or made) you feel so intimidated? Should you feel intimidated by them?

5. Is there anything important or valuable that intimidation or fear has kept you from doing? Does it still keep you from doing this?

6. Can you think of a time when fear and/or intimidation has kept you from moving forward or standing up against something difficult or wrong?

7. What would your life be like if fear and intimidation were not factors?

8. Can you identify any negative forces or decisions in your life to which you need to stand up and "just say no"?

9. What would it take for you to say no to every force in your life that holds you back? Are you willing to pray to the Lord for the strength to do so? Are you willing to keep praying this, defying those bullying forces on a daily basis? What do you think would happen if you did?

CHAPTER 3

Why I Hate to be Naked
Disarming Grace

In you they trusted and were not put to shame.
Psalm 22:5

OUR STORY

Think back with me for a moment to seventh grade. Many of us remember feeling a certain squeamishness while walking through the halls between classes. As we began searching for that true identity that hid somewhere amidst those awkward growth spurts and unnerving hormonal surges, we also began struggling to figure out what it was we truly wanted in life.

We wanted the beautiful people to laugh with us as we told a great joke or did an awesome stunt. More likely we held back for fear that they would laugh at us, noticing our messed-up hair or the new pimple strategically placed right in the center of our nose. We wanted to be the one who wore the latest, boldest clothing trends. We also feared that if our fashion choices got too daring, they would all label us the freak or the bogus dresser.

Many of us wanted to feel special, to stand out as one of the popular crowd. But we held back, for fear that we would stick out, appearing un-cool in the slightest way. In an era where we so needed to assert our own individuality and identity, we also felt that strong pull to blend into the crowd, to stick with the status quo.

This profound and uneasy distress we felt had nothing to do with our own personal, inherent awkwardness. Or rather, it had everything to do with it. We were all geeks back then. Some of us just showed more outward evidence of it than others. Even the beautiful, popular ones struggled behind their apparent confidence.

Like the rest of us, they still asked the same questions about their worth. Does anyone love me for who I am? Am I really a valuable person? Do I really deserve to take up space? They wanted to stand out and feared sticking out. They just covered it up a little better than the rest of us.

Thus began the initial birth pains of adult living.

Most of us still deal with this inner awkwardness, this intense non-comfort within our own skin. We still fear that others will judge us as harshly as we judge ourselves. With time we just get better at covering it up, like some of the popular people in middle school.

MY STORY

Nowhere did this uncomfortable pre-adolescent reality strike me more than in gym class, in the locker room to be precise. Ladies, remember that one girl who could never get dressed in front of the others? (Gentlemen, I am not sure if you had one of those, but I suspect such.) She always grabbed her clothes and ran to a restroom stall to change. She may have even gotten to class a couple of minutes early, so no one would notice her—well—differentness. You always wondered what she had to hide.

I was that girl.

My physical modesty had nothing to do with any natural shyness. I cannot remember a time when I was ever really afraid to speak my mind as needed. Talking to complete strangers never fazed me in the least. In most ways, I did not even mind sticking out in the crowd, even as a junior high student. Years later upon taking a personality test, I scored 59 on a scale of 1 to 65 in extroversion. I simply hated to be naked in front of other people.

So, what did I have to hide? *Everything*! My unworthy undergarments never matched up to the crowd of training bras and lacy bikini briefs. My "leftover baby fat," as I heard some family members call it, rather stuck out amidst the rest of the girls, whose height had overtaken any previous forms of grammar school chubbiness. (I never did outgrow that baby fat.)

Then came the dreaded swimming classes. Not even my undergarments could help me then. Oh, to have had the ability to bring my personal shower from home, the one that actually had a shower curtain. Fortunately, I still had the trusty old bathroom stall to save me from my shame.

Eventually I worked up the nerve to start changing within the general locker room population. There I noticed that though not everyone hid quite as fully as me, some girls got dressed much, much more quickly than others, and some even moved to their own row of lockers to do so. It helped to know that others too suffered from this double ailment of both bodily imperfection and the self-conscious awareness of it.

I so envied the beautiful ones, the locker room royalty. They would prance around in their superior, lacy skivvies without a hint of shame. Yes, it must have been their undergarments that gave them the power of self-confidence, and it worked even when they had their clothes on. These were the same ones who ruled the school, walking about the halls with the confidence of queens.

My extreme bodily reserve did let up a bit as I progressed into high school. By that point in my life, I simply didn't care if other girls didn't like my figure or my underclothes. I figured out that I probably should not worry about the opinion of the type of girl who would take the time to study me in that state anyhow. (That said, if I really thought another girl took the time to look at me that closely while I changed, I probably *would* have moved back to the bathroom stall.)

I also realized by then that the other ladies were too worried about their own bodies to be paying any sort of close attention to anyone else's, namely mine.

Of course, I still felt horrified at the thought of bearing anything private in front of members of the opposite sex. To me they represented another whole level of judgment and loneliness. Many of them represented a potential mate, whose rejection could mean a lifetime of isolation and despair. That fear kept me out of a lot of trouble.

I showed my concern in a rather militant manner. While I have never condemned violence for its own sake, I was extremely vocal about my willingness to hurt any guy who even thought about touching me the wrong way. A few unwise gentlemen who chose to test me in this area discovered that this dog's bite was as strong as her bark. In retrospect, it amazes me that I had any male friends at all, but generally those who dared to even come anywhere near me kept their hands off.

Things changed when I got married. At first, I held a similar reserve to exposing my imperfections to even my husband, Ben. However, I soon realized that he sought to accept and embrace everything about me, warts and all. He wanted the chance to see the hidden parts of me, good and bad so that he could appreciate and love them too. Amazingly, he even kept loving me as I put on extra weight after giving birth.

I came to realize that some of the things that I considered imperfections, he saw as endearing characteristics. This all made sense to me because I felt the same way about him. Our bodies only scratched the surface of this mutual self-revelation.

I noticed that as we grew more comfortable with one another as "one flesh," we simultaneously grew more comfortable with ourselves as individuals. Perhaps this is because the more we have learned how to be together, the better we have become at being ourselves.

Even more so, as we have experienced this broken human version of unconditional love, we have come to realize just how much more our Heavenly Father's infinite and perfect love and acceptance reaches into the depths of our being. With this new awareness, we need not fear rejection.

Our journey together has included far more rocky terrain than I could share in one book. I feel certain that we have faced several seasons wherein we would not have made it without the grace of God and a good deal of prayer. However, the struggle has yielded exceedingly more benefits than difficulties.

For one thing, I can finally stand to be naked and unashamed, before both God and Ben.

GOD'S STORY

Picture this. You literally live in the ultimate paradise without a care in the world, wanting for absolutely nothing. Then some dumb snake (or actually a rather smart one) comes along and tricks you into believing that more does exist, and that it's yours for the picking.

One bite later you immediately notice something missing. Everything looks the same, and at the same time completely different. It takes no real search to find the cause. *You* are the cause. *You* have changed. So, you do the first thing you can think of doing to mask that inherent "wrongness" that you sense but cannot define.

I still find it somewhat odd that at the point where Adam and Eve pretty much botched the course of all human history, the first thought on their minds revolved around what clothes they would wear. I myself have never really equated sin with a fashion crisis. This seems even stranger when one considers that clothes did not even exist before that moment.

This begs the question, how could they come to feel such shame about their lack of covering when every living creature had existed without clothing every moment from the beginning of time until then? I would think that if anything they would want to hide their mouths, the sinful perpetrators, rather than their other parts.

A biblical understanding of nakedness and shame sheds some light on this matter. Shame, in the scriptural sense, reaches far beyond our modern sense of embarrassing guilt. It combines a deep-seated remorse over past mistakes, or even the appearance of mistakes, with a far-reaching apprehension over how others might use our weaknesses against us. With mistakes and imperfections comes defeat, and with defeat come the possibilities of exploitation, judgment, and loss.

To this end, shame has as much and sometimes more to do with the world around us as it has to do with ourselves. For this reason, alcoholics and un-wed mothers no longer feel the same level of shame that they once did. This can act as a catalyst to recovery, as compassionate helpers and friends support them with the understanding that no one lives without sin or flaw. Indeed, we as God's children are all called to live by the rules of mercy and forgiveness. However, it can also pave the road to destruction, as the absence of any fear of offending God or immediate retribution leads them to dig deeper and deeper into a pit of despair.

On the other hand, our pluralistic society often compels us to feel shame about holding to certain standards of God-honoring living. Some equate virginity or chastity with naiveté, lack of experience, or the inability to get a date. People who abstain from excessive alcohol or gambling often strike the less restrained as boring or prudish. Those of you who choose to exercise these godly virtues of personal restraint, I encourage you to always hold your head high without fear or shame. Look forward to God's harvest for those who choose to never give up on doing good (Galatians 6:9).

Just as shame has to do with more than ourselves, the biblical meaning of nakedness has to do with more than mere physical nudity. It means complete and full exposure, without armor or protection.

The apparent defenselessness that accompanies nakedness only alarms us when we sense the possibility of attack. Most of us do not cower in embarrassment or constantly look over our shoulders while taking a shower or changing in our bedrooms. In those situations, we generally have no reason to fear attack, harm, or exploitation. However, it serves us well to limit our physical exposure in a snowstorm by piling on layers of clothes, or to remain properly dressed in rooms full of people who will not honor our intimate areas the way our spouses do.

In the case of Adam and Eve, shame over their nakedness had little to do with their apparent lack of clothing. Rather, eating the fruit made them aware of the mess they had created. They covered the outside as an attempt to shield the inner brokenness. They masked their bodies in an attempt to hide their hearts.

That forbidden fruit gave Adam and Eve new knowledge all right. Today we call it fear. When the Bible says that Adam and Eve noticed their nakedness, it does not refer to their sudden awareness of an apparel deficiency. Rather, they sensed the imminent danger that their mistake had caused them. They desperately covered their bodies with fig leaves in an effort to protect themselves from the consequences of their own poor judgment.

Satan seduced them into believing this lie: that going against God's will would leave them better off than obedience. God did not originally grant them the awareness of possible harm because, before they sinned, that danger did not exist. The serpent craftily twisted the truth of this statement to make bad seem good and dark seem light.

Such is the draw of all worldly lust. You see, without a cause for shame, there is no reason to fear nakedness. Put another way, 1 John 4:18 states, "There is no fear in love. But perfect love drives out fear, because fear has to do with punishment. The one who fears is not made perfect in love."

Nowadays nakedness means different things to different people. To expose a person's shady past, secret desires, or hidden weakness often causes people far greater embarrassment than merely revealing various body parts.

Our covering also comes in different shapes and forms. Ironically, some people actually use nudity as a form of "clothing," as they bear their bodies in a futile effort to further shield their broken hearts.

In many cases, humility and discretion serve us well. God does not intend for us to purposely open ourselves up for non-stop, needless attack. Indiscriminately exposing ourselves to such would reflect great foolishness.

However, we also show great wisdom in remembering that certain times call for our return to the pre-sin Eden. As relationships with friends and family deepen, we may enjoy that great intimacy that well-spent vulnerability can bring about. When we meet and marry our romantic match, we gradually learn to reveal our deeper selves, to both ourselves and our mate, and we may begin to learn the meaning of unconditional love from another human being.

Most importantly, with God we need never fear nakedness. With every confession, every tear of brokenness, our heavenly fortress will only expand those infinite arms of grace, showing us over and over again what perfect agape love truly means.

That said, to this day I still don't care much for the locker room scene.

> *Lord*, thank you for loving every part of me, warts and all. I know that in you I have a safe place to be my truest self. God, I know that sometimes I hold back, which has more to do with my own self-judgment than with your uncon- ditional love. Help me to learn to stand naked in your presence without fear, knowing that you will never harm or exploit my open brokenness. You will only love and heal my exposed and wounded soul.

YOUR STORY

Read and reflect upon Genesis 2:25–3:21. Then consider the follow- ing questions:

1. What or whom do you think Adam and Eve feared after they ate the forbidden fruit? Why do you think they feared?

2. Think about the connection between nakedness and shame in the Garden of Eden. What caused Adam and Eve to feel so ashamed of their nakedness?

3. What makes you feel naked and exposed? Do you have anything about yourself that you will hide from people at all costs?

4. Have you ever had a friend or family member that inspired total vulnerability in you? If so, what characteristic in him/her caused you to feel so comfortable in your openness? If not, what characteristics would a person need to have in order to make you feel that way?

5. Do you feel comfortable being naked before God? If not, what keeps you from feeling this way?

6. How does it make you feel to know that the Lord sees you fully, even when you do not choose to reveal yourself?

CHAPTER 4

PUTTING GOD ON TRIAL
Misunderstood Grace

*A person's own folly leads to their ruin, yet their heart rages
against the Lord.*
Proverbs 19:3

OUR STORY

"I love it when a plan comes together." Hannibal, a character on
the 1980s series *The A-Team*, made this phrase famous. He would
gloatingly say this at the end of almost every episode as his team
completed some nearly impossible feat.

Unlike the A-team, most of us do not know the privilege of
having every project in our lives work out the way we plan. In fact,
few of our plans do. Some of us (especially parents with small children
in the house) feel accomplished on those days we are able to even
make it out the front door without having some small crisis drive a
rift through our best made plans.

This rings true from the minutest detail, like a recipe gone wrong
or a foul ball in a baseball game, to the grandest conception. For some,
it can extend through the course of their lifetimes. So many people
look back on the flood of years they have lived in great amazement,
thinking, "This is not the life I thought I would have."

Two extremes can define humanity's reactions to such trials. At one extreme, people who are at their best receive these disappointments as a blessed opportunity to grow in grace. They recognize God's hand in both the good and bad. If others do something to cause them harm, to bring about this change of plans, these people have the faith to say, "What humans meant for bad, God meant for good" (Genesis 15:20, author's paraphrase). They also find the personal grace to forgive, which sets their hearts free.

If they make a mistake to alter their own life's course, some even find the grace to forgive themselves, and they recognize that God uses even their missteps to shape their character and teach them. In fact, when something unexpectedly bad happens to people, the best of them begin their analysis of the situation by praising God and checking their own hearts.

When circumstances over which they have no control alter the course of their lives, these people will struggle just like the rest of us. They also question God, like so many of us—only they have a different question. While most of us ask, "God, why are you doing this?" these people of deeper faith say, "God, I know you can use this for your glory and my good." They seek God's face first and foremost before asking for God's hand.

Others react in the exact opposite manner. When faced with the unexpected and unpleasant curveballs of life, they will fuss, kick, moan, mope, or wallow in self-pity. "Woe is me," they say while looking over a life of regret and remorse. Sometimes the only difference between a life of great success and one of depressing failure lies in the eye of the beholder.

Some people inflict their own self-injury by replaying the past wrongs done to them over and over again in their heads, freshly wounding themselves with circumstances from years and even decades past. Some reclaim defeat over victories that God has already won. They do not realize that until they let the past go, they will not be able to move forward into God's best life for them.

When they experience a change or crisis that they cannot blame on another person, they often choose to blame God or themselves. They do not necessarily admit this on the surface. They carry the anger deep inside them, often completely flipping it inward in the form of depression.

Satan cleverly disguises some forms of self-pity as guilt. This guilt has nothing to do with the conviction of the Holy Spirit, though Satan would have you think that they are the same. God's conviction will always push us forward and through. Satan's guilt leaves us festering and wallowing in self-disgust, a sort of spiritual quicksand that will drown our hearts if we do not take care to stand against it.

Some people do so well at rehearsing the role of victim that they can only see the harm that they believe others have done to them. Some get so angry at what they see as "the wrong," that they fail to ever take ownership of their role in it. They sometimes even write false villains into their life's stage, blaming people who have nothing to do with the situation.

In truth, most of us believers have a little bit of each kind of person in us. We can find at least a little silver lining in some things, and we have known days where despair seemed far closer than hope.

We can also think of certain people who lean a lot closer to the first type of person than the second. I wish I could say I'm more like the first. I must shamefully admit that as much as I love a good comedy, I often become too attached to the drama of my own suffering. When I don't get what I want, I sometimes try to make myself feel better by playing the role of martyr, indulging myself in a victim mentality.

Thank the Lord that God will meet us exactly where we are at. As we come to God openly and honestly with whatever we feel, God will be faithful to walk us through it all, and even to work it all for our good. Thank the Lord that God's grace extends beyond our attitudes of misguided understanding.

MY STORY

God seemed to work overtime addressing my addiction to control and self-indulgence during my college years. My junior year in particular began with a symphony of drama, complete with the high notes of excitement and the percussive beatings of disappointment.

My first apartment far exceeded all of my expectations or hopes. Occupying the entire third floor of an old grand Victorian mansion, it came complete with three bedrooms, a huge walk-in closet, a washer and dryer, and a great view of the small town in which I lived. I felt like I lived in a castle. The rent was an astoundingly small $350 a month. (Over the following decade I paid as much as three times that amount for considerably less space.)

I had also just made a down-payment on a sensible, low-mileage car, my very first personal vehicle. This was all within walking distance from the church where I would work part-time when not attending classes at my school fifteen miles away. Yes, my life was coming together quite nicely.

It mattered little to me that I had no clue of how I was going to pay for it all. I felt that God had provided me this apartment and car, and I just knew that the Lord would provide me the money to pay for them.

I saw this as a glorious leap of faith on my part. Besides, there had to be some place in town that would hire me, to make up for the financial difference where my first job fell short. If nothing else, I could just take out another student loan. From my best calculations, this would not be necessary, since the cost of the car and apartment together equaled much less than the price of a dorm and the board plan at the expensive private college I attended.

A few days after signing the lease I got a note in the mail from the housing director at school. She needed to know about my housing plans for the year, for her records. I had already sent her the required form with my housing plans the previous spring. I figured that she must have misplaced it. No big deal. So, I gave her a quick call.

"Karen, who approved your off-campus living plans," she said quite crossly.

"I sent you the official form with my housing plans last spring. You never told me that this would not work."

She seemed indignant. "Had I seen a note like that, I would never have approved it. And common sense should tell you that the absence of a disapproval note does not mean approval."

"I'm a junior. I didn't think anyone needed to approve them."

"The student handbook"—a two-hundred-page, small-print document—"clearly states the guidelines. I cannot believe that you did not consult it for this. Students cannot live off campus without permission unless they are married, living with family, or over twenty-five. That's against our policy."

"Okay, who do I ask for permission?"

"There are only a certain number of junior students who are able to live off campus in *approved* housing. All of those slots have been taken, and your apartment is not approved housing."

I was beginning to see the value of state schools. No one there got a hard time for getting their own place.

"But I already signed a lease," I blurted out, dazed and bewildered.

"That was *very* unwise. Whether or not you have signed that lease, you are still bound by our rules to pay for a dorm and the board plan." Those costs equaled almost twice the amount of that year's lease.

"I can't afford to do that."

"Well, you don't have much of a choice."

I felt my blood begin to boil. Could this even be legal? For Heaven's sake, I was an adult, and a student in good standing. Could they really tell me where I could and could not live?

What on earth was I going to do? I was locked into a lease for this apartment with no out clause, and I had just made a large, non-refundable down-payment for a car. I was at the end of my financial resources, and I literally had no money left to pay for tuition if I paid for a dorm and the college meal plan. On the other hand, they would not let me register for classes without doing so. I was stuck.

After about an hour of motionless shock, I began a frenzy of desperate phone calls. First, I called my pastor. She had some authority with the college. Perhaps she could plead my case and change their minds. No such luck.

When this did not work, I called my uncle and aunt, who lived in a nearby town. Remembering that the rules permitted us to live with family off campus, I thought maybe, just maybe, they could let me claim residency at their house while I lived in the apartment. I was ashamed to even ask, and I shuddered at the dishonesty of the words coming out of my mouth. But perhaps, I reasoned, since they were pastors, they could somehow anoint the idea and change it into something holy, like ministers change bread into Christ's spiritual body for communion. Obviously, no such luck. What was I thinking?

Next, I called the youth and young-adult pastor from my church. There was not much that she could do, but if nothing else, I could ramble, scream, complain, and cry at will, and she would understand. Honestly, I think I scared her a little, as she had never seen me that worked up.

Ultimately, I knew what phone call I really needed to make. I had to swallow my pride and call my father, who had discouraged me from getting my own apartment from the beginning. It almost felt like he had willed for me to fail, and I just knew that he would be waiting on the other end of the line to say "I told you so. How could you be so foolish?"

With great fear and anguish, I finally called home. I stayed on the phone with Mom as long as I possibly could before asking for my father, bracing myself for the lecture of my life. To my astonishment, he only said two sentences: "You need to come home? I'll be there to pick you up tomorrow." Without a single word of judgment, Mom and Dad made the ten-hour round trip to pick me up the next day, showing nothing but love and relief for my well-being as they brought me home.

Mom even seemed a little excited to welcome me home to my room in their new place. I suspect she had been worried about me, and she felt relieved that I would have a place to stay.

I would like to say that my parents' response convinced me of God's provision, and that my heart overflowed with gratitude for their understanding and support at that point. In reality, I was too mad at God, and afraid for the future, to feel anything good for anyone else.

After all, the whole plan to live off campus was supposed to be for God's glory. I was to be more involved in my church, reach out more to the lost, and study and serve more to prepare myself for ministry.

I thought that because of God, I was stuck paying a year's lease for a home in which I could not even live, I would surely lose my car deposit, and my two years of tuition and study was going down the drain, as I was forced to withdraw from classes. Within a two-day period I went from having my own home, job, car, and future to the state of a penniless, degree-less, jobless, pathetic mess.

How dare God mess up my plans for serving the Lord like that! Forget serving God wholeheartedly. I was not even sure I wanted God around. I felt like I needed a vacation from my own beliefs.

I have always believed in being honest with the Lord in my prayers. After all, God knows what I am thinking already, so I might as well fess up. My heart spewed forth an overflow of brutal honesty with the Lord that evening, to the point of cruelty.

In a sense, I put God on trial that night for the hurt I had suffered. Acting as plaintiff, judge, and jury, I convicted the Lord of failure to meet my needs. The sentence would be that God just had to put up with my complaining, sulking, and angry spirit for as long as I felt like moping around.

Most people have experienced the awkwardness of witnessing a public temper tantrum from a young child who does not receive his or her desires. Similarly, my thoughts and actions towards my heavenly Daddy in the following days would have been enough to make decent people blush. It is a wonder that the Lord did not strike me down with lightning given the disrespect that I showed.

Nevertheless, Daddy God showed calmness and patience with me, holding me in his arms like a parent holds an inconsolable child who just cannot seem to understand. Though I stood as the true defendant in this case, my God never did stop meeting my needs.

I lived with my parents for the next year and found a job back home to pay off my expenses. Miraculously, the car dealership refunded my down-payment. Also, after a few months of my paying rent, the owner of the house found a new tenant and released me from the lease.

My enrollment in the local community college kept my coursework up to date, while avoiding the high cost of that year in a private college. The next year I returned to my private school as a senior, in approved housing this time. By God's grace I even graduated on time, despite my own foolishness. God knew what he was doing after all. Not even my own imperfections could thwart the Lord's plan for my good.

GOD'S STORY

I can relate to the joy and exuberance King David must have felt during the holy parade in which the Israelites brought the Ark of the Covenant into Jerusalem. Thousands upon thousands of people lined up along the route to see the procession. What a glorious sight, to see God's people move in perfect harmony around the literal housing case of God's presence, the Ark of the Covenant holding the Ten Commandments.

I can also imagine David's surprise, anger, and dismay when the Lord struck down one of his men in the midst of the celebration and worship. How horribly unjust God must have seemed, to kill someone who was actually trying to protect the ark from falling. When the ark began to shake, Uzzah, one of the men guiding the cart that carried the ark, quickly thought to reach out and steady it to prevent it from falling. "The Lord's anger burned against Uzzah, and he struck him down because he had put his hand on the ark. So he died there before God" (1 Chronicles 13:10).

David must have mentally scolded the Lord for choosing to (in David's mind) unjustly put to death a faithful servant precisely at the point where they were preparing to enter Jerusalem, a city whose very name means *peace* in Hebrew. By all earthly standards, Uzzah should have received a reward, not a burial. How could God bring such unmerited tragedy on a day meant for celebration, a day meant for celebration of *God*?

David, the earthly authority in the land, put God on trial, acting as prosecutor, judge, and jury. His verdict was a resounding guilty to murder in the first degree, not to mention the misdemeanors of disturbing the peace and contemptible behavior against the king.

The sentence? Silence. David responded by saying nothing and trying to get away from God. He left the ark, a symbol of the Lord's presence, at a nearby house, and he kept going. Obviously, leaving the Ark of the Covenant did no real harm to God, and it brought real blessings to the household of people who watched over it in the king's absence. David's lashing out at God hurt no one but himself.

In truth, the blood of Uzzah was on David's head. David had probably tried to use the ark as political leverage to strengthen his earthly position as king. Given the location and context from which the ark had been moved, Uzzah was most likely directly kin to Saul, the former king of Israel (1 Samuel 7:1; 2 Samuel 6:3). To honor Saul's memory by allowing one of his kinsmen to guide the ark would surely solidify peace and support from the entire tribe of Benjamin, Saul's tribe.

Whatever David's plans or motives were, his choice of Uzzah to guide the Ark of the Covenant directly countered God's will. In the book of law, God had clearly stated that only the Levites, the anointed, direct descendants of Levi, should carry the Ark of the Covenant. Had David followed God's instructions, the whole nation would have been safer.

As is always the case, God's rules came for everyone's protection, and yet David chose to disregard them. Things worked out against David's will because David had acted against God's will.

It took some time for David to open his eyes, but God showed great patience. After a while David realized that he had tried to hold God accountable to his own faulty human reasoning, rather than taking steps to hold himself accountable to God (1 Chronicles 15:13).

When David finally wised up to the truth, he showed that he had learned his lesson. In recognition of his mistake, David made a public decree ordering that only the Levites, God's chosen people to carry the

Ark of the Covenant, would go near it. This echoed God's own earlier decrees through the prophet Moses. David also made a careful census of the Levites, to ensure the proper treatment of the ark.

God had every right and power to self-vindicate in response to David's anger and accusations. Instead, in an act of truly divine grace, the Lord waited patiently as David worked through his feelings.

Unlike most of us, God never seems preoccupied with thoughts of either self-defense or self-vindication. After all, the Lord Jesus endured an insanely unjust trial, multiple beatings, and the most brutal form of death, all for the ultimate good of the very people who struck Him.

Like David, I also eventually woke up to the myriad of my own mistakes that had led me to this point of financial crisis. Most notably, I had ignored the advice of most of my family and friends. There was also that little issue of my failure to read the school handbook.

When I finally opened my eyes to this reality, my call to God brought forth a similar response as the phone call I had made to my parents. There were no words of condemnation. No finger pointing or lectures about my irresponsibility. There were only open arms from a loving parent who was happy to welcome me back home.

> *Lord*, I praise you for your relentless love that holds on through my doubts, fears, and misunderstandings. Grant me the grace, Lord, to love with that kind of patience and perseverance when others misunderstand.

YOUR STORY

Read and reflect upon 1 Chronicles 13:1–12, 15:1–2. Then consider the following questions:

1. Did David have a good reason to be angry with God? Why or why not?

2. What did God do in response to David's anger? What did God *not* do in response to David's anger?

3. Can you think of a time or circumstance of extreme injustice, when you or someone you love suffered in ways they did not deserve? When this happened, did you blame anyone for this? Are you still living in this circumstance? Do you blame anyone for this?

4. Have you ever blamed God for something that was your fault, or some other human's fault? Have you ever blamed God for something that was no one's fault? How did you get past it?

5. How willing do you think God is to listen to our heart's cry when it is full of anger, particularly anger at God? Does God stop listening to us when we express our negative emotions? How important is it for us to be honest with God when we are angry? Explain.

6. Can you think of a time in your life where seeking and listening to God, along with the advice of others, would have saved you time, money, or heartache?

CHAPTER 5

Waking Up to Glory
Inconvenient Grace

*My flesh and my heart may fail, but God is the strength of my heart
and my portion forever.*
Psalm 73:26

OUR STORY

Life presents us with a series of opportunities that fall within a certain continuum on our list of desires and priorities. In other words, we would much rather do some things than others.

At one extreme we have our dreams. It seems we would give just about anything to experience certain things. I for instance, would almost kill for the chance to see my name on *The New York Times*'s best-seller list. (So please recommend this book to all your friends—your life depends on it.) Others would give their right arm to eat in a certain restaurant, meet a certain person, or travel to a certain place.

Then we have those readily available opportunities for daily joy: a walk in the park with a loved one, a hard-earned vacation, or a Saturday morning cuddle session with our beloved daughter and husband. (The last one is my favorite.) We try to plan for such occasions, and yet the best times often come when we least expect them.

In the middle we have those opportunities that we could pretty much do with or without, what I call the "whatever" opportunities.

"Hey, Honey, do you want to rent a movie?" Whatever. "Would you mind leading the opening hymn in church today?" Whatever. "Ma'am, would you mind taking our picture while we stand in front of this statue?" Whatever. Of course, we do not usually answer that way out loud, but those words reflect our attitude on many of these occasions. It really does not matter to us either way.

Toward the bottom of the continuum, we have the "I'd rather not, but . . ." category. Some of us prefer not to wear bathing suits, but we will in a heartbeat if going swimming means bringing a smile to the faces of our children or grandchildren. Certain people simply do not enjoy exercise, but they will go to the gym regularly so that they stay in shape. Many children abhor the thought of cleaning their rooms, but they (I should say some of them) will do so to gain their allowance money or avoid punishment.

At the bottom of our list, we all have those "only if I have to" experiences. We hate to do them, but we have no choice. Many of us share a common list of this category for which procrastination was invented, including homework, housework, changing diapers, and getting out of bed on our day off. This also includes talking to the person you generally avoid, filling out that tedious paperwork needed in order for you to get the raise, and eating that awful health food without which you may suffer another heart attack.

Two more important categories lie off our mental charts in both extremes, because in most cases they do not even cross our minds. Beyond the positive extreme lie those experiences which far exceed our wildest dreams. I cannot even list these things because they exceed imagination. We only know of them when they happen. If we feel the unbelievable blessing of experiencing these moments even once in our lifetimes, they completely blow our minds and rock our worlds.

On the other hand, we have the "heck, no!" category, otherwise known as the "never in a million years—you would have to tie me down and kill me first" category. These are precisely the things that we do not think about when we wholeheartedly commit to going anywhere that God sends us. If we thought about them in church, we would change the words of the classic hymns to "*almost* anywhere He leads me, I will follow" and "I surrender *most*."

Because God is God, sometimes the very situations that we most fear and detest become a catalyst for experiencing God's glory beyond our wildest dreams. In this space of holy providence, sometimes the far-reaching extremes work together to show us God's greatness and provision. In other words, when we face the "absolutely not" situations, and then we do them anyhow, we sometimes find ourselves blessed beyond our wildest imaginations. If you have ever experienced this, you know exactly what I mean.

MY STORY

Lana embodied the epitome of my "Heck, no!" situation. She was without a doubt the most unpleasant person I had ever met. Everything she said seemed to come out with spit and venom. Heaven forbid that anyone should ever ask how she was doing; she stood ever and all too willing to tell with great detail how awful life was treating her.

I thought of myself as a friendly, outgoing person who could strike a comfortable friendship with about anyone, but Lana single-handedly proved me wrong. I could never seem to get her to be pleasant with me, or even to smile.

So, I developed a certain policy for dealing with her. While around her, I would go out of my way to be kind, cordial, and pleasant. And whenever possible, I avoided her like the plague.

To be honest, I do not know why she even bothered coming to the youth and young-adult retreat that weekend. She did not seem to like any of us there, and for the most part, we returned the sentiment. More accurately, most of us tried not to pay much attention to her at all. We all knew what she was like, and we spent too little time together to waste our energy on what struck us as a lost cause.

It seemed appropriate that dark clouds started forming in the sky when Lana approached on the Saturday evening of the retreat. In my usual fashion I exchanged a few friendly words, as I looked for the opportunity to politely excuse myself to go somewhere else—anywhere else.

Unfortunately, before I could get away, Lana made eye contact and began speaking directly to me. Suddenly I felt trapped. I saw no way out of what was bound to be yet another pessimistic conversation with the queen of morbidity. I quickly fastened my mental seatbelt and braced myself for another whirlwind ride on the gloomsmobile.

The dark clouds thickened, and Lana did not disappoint. She proceeded to share some random tales about the people she knew who had cast evil spells that really worked, and about others who had been demon-possessed and struck down in other ways by evil spirits. She shared with great intensity as some of the younger members of our circle listened wide-eyed and amazed at her satanic tales. Some even joined in with myths and urban legends of their own.

Within a few minutes the sky turned pitch black as the ever-thickening storm clouds covered the moon. Had it not been for a couple of outdoor lights, we would not have been able to see a thing. I sensed the imminent storm. At that point I welcomed the excuse to run indoors, away from Lana's web of evil.

Honestly, I could not believe her nerve. What place did talk of demon-possession have at this *Christian* retreat? It was as if she had come just to sabotage what goodness and beauty the Lord had in store for the rest of us. From a very early age I felt quite strongly about the realms of witchcraft and demon-possession. I cringed at the thought of countless Christians who treated the dark arts as something fun and entertaining, even playing with satanic instruments (such as tarot cards and Ouija boards) like toys.

Obviously, I would need to temporarily cast aside my policy of pleasantness, quite easily replacing it with a strong dose of self-righteousness. When I could take it no longer, I finally spoke up. "I just don't understand why you guys are talking like this. Don't you realize how strong the realm of evil is? It is not something to be taken lightly like this."

At that comment, the whole camp seemed to fall silent as all eyes focused on me. So much for my plan to dodge the conversation. I imagine that my friends thought the passion in my voice came from some holy desire within me to share the truth with them. Honestly,

I was just thoroughly annoyed about my present incarceration in this least desirable environment. It was precisely at that point when the Lord chose to use me.

I continued, without quite understanding what came out of my mouth:

"We are doing exactly what Satan wants us to do. He wants us to be preoccupied with his power. You know, I read somewhere that Christians can make two opposite but equal mistakes about the power of evil. We can ignore it, allowing it to creep in and take over our lives, keeping us from God's power. Or we can become obsessed with it, allowing it to trick us into giving up God's power and protection that is available to us."

"That makes a lot of sense," remarked one of my younger friends.

Without thought, I kept going. "The thing is, as powerful as Satan is, God is so much more powerful. We alone can't stand up to evil. But when we allow God to live in us, Satan doesn't stand a chance against us. You see, we will always be possessed by something. Something will always own us. But when the Holy Spirit possesses us, completely, then there's no room left for evil. They simply can't co-exist." This all sounded really good to me, and the words were true. But upon reflection I know that what came out of my mouth did not reflect the dark feelings of judgment and rage that my heart bore at the start of the conversation. However, somewhere between the beginning and the end of those statements, God worked a miracle.

I cannot explain, nor can I even remember, the specific details of the conversation that followed over the next two hours. In a sense, my soul retreated from consciousness, and in my absence, the Holy Spirit took over. What I do remember is that two hours later we were all singing praise songs, and the clouds had disappeared to reveal a perfectly clear, moonlit night. We experienced a mini-Pentecost![3]

---

3 Pentecost refers to what happened in Acts 2, when the Holy Spirit first came to the young believers, and miraculous things happened. Many count it as the birth of the Christian church.

Most miraculously, I saw a genuine smile on Lana's face for the first time ever in my four years knowing her. That night she met with Jesus. With Christ in her life, she instantly became a different person, a friend. The next day, my new friend shared this with me: "There have been other times when I asked Jesus to be my Savior with my lips, because some adult told me that I had to. But every time I did, I was really cursing God and telling him I hated him in my heart. I blamed the Lord for all of the hurt that my family has gone through. But now I know the truth. It's not God's fault that my family has suffered. He's been wanting to help me all along. And now I know Jesus."

The excitement in her voice escalated as tears started to well up in her eyes. "I mean, I *really* know Jesus, and I feel his love. And for the very first time in my life, I am truly happy. I can't stop smiling. Only Jesus could make me feel this way. I can't believe I wasted so much time hating God."

Was this the same girl that I couldn't stand to be around twelve hours ago? What an unbelievable change! Next Lana made the most shocking comment of all: "Jesus used you to bring me salvation last night. I thank God that you were willing to share this love with me. It has changed my life."

I bowed my heart in both humility and gratitude that God would choose to shine through the cracks of my broken perspective. At the beginning of the previous night, I felt cornered, forced to stay against my will. Little did I know that God had done the cornering, inescapably backing me into the blessing of God's grace.

GOD'S STORY

Sometimes when I read about Jesus's life, I get very frustrated with the disciples. How could they walk the earth with God in the flesh for three years and yet have been so completely clueless about his divine identity?

The most vivid example of this spiritual blindness appears in the book of Luke, in what we call Jesus Christ's Transfiguration. At that moment, God's glory showed around Jesus so intensely that he literally glowed, and one could hear the voice of God from Heaven quite clearly claiming Christ as God's Son.

So, what did Peter and his friends do during all of this? *They fell asleep*! The Maker of the universe took his closest earthly friends to experience God Incarnate's glory, and they did not even want to be there! They wanted to be in bed.

Could this be the same Peter who only a week before openly recognized Jesus as God's chosen one to free Israel, the most important hero of all time?

Could these be the same ordinary men whom Christ had recently empowered to do extraordinary things, like heal the sick, cast out demons, and even raise the dead (Matthew 10:8)? What other group in history was able to feel such a rush of God's power?

How could they think about the physical need for rest while in the presence of God's Holy One, who could meet such basic needs as food for more than five thousand people from a small boy's humble lunch? Had I been in the presence of such greatness, sleep would have been the last thing on my mind. I would be wide awake on the edge of my seat waiting to receive whatever amazing thing would come next.

Then again, how easy it must have been to take Jesus's greatness for granted as they walked with him every single day for three years. Though the Bible instructs us to pray without ceasing (1 Thessalonians 5:17), a long day's work can easily leave many with the more difficult task, to pray without *sleeping*.

Such was the case with the disciples. They were exhausted. They were human. In an act of divine grace, the Lord chose to shine down on them in glory precisely at their weakest point.

On that journey up the mountain with Jesus, the worn-out Peter may have wished that the Christ would have asked another disciple to take the tiring walk with Him. However, the important thing is not how he and the others went up the mountain, but how they came down. He went back a changed man forever. The greatest miracle came not in the transfiguration of Christ's body, but in the transformation of these three disciples' hearts.

Unfortunately, this did not mark that last time the disciples would fail to pay attention to God's call. Within months the religious authorities wrongfully arrested and tried Jesus. Rather than going after him, most of the disciples just ran away.

Peter at least followed, though he did so under the cover of night. And when the moment of truth came, when people asked him if he knew Christ, he failed miserably. When given the chance to stand up and speak for his very best friend Jesus, Peter vehemently denied even knowing him . . . three times!

Ironically, the Lord even used Peter's betrayal to bring about God's glory. Once again, God's grace and sovereignty did not just work *despite* human failure—it worked right through it. Not only did Christ's death lead to life for all who would receive, but the conviction and restoration in Peter after this failure led him to speak more boldly and fearlessly for his Lord throughout the rest of his life. In a sense, his momentary deep spiritual sleep led to a greater, more glorious awakening.

I was a lot like Peter on the night of Lana's salvation. While I may not have actually closed my eyes and rested, I certainly fell asleep on the job. Yet God both used me and blessed me. When I became fully awake, I experienced God's glory, that awesome and all-consuming experience to which we can respond in no other way but to fall on our knees and worship the Holy One.

What happened on that night at the retreat did not happen because of my faithfulness, my desire, my worthiness, or even because of my availability. None of those were present in me at the time. What happened was purely from God's glory, through God's glory, and to God's glory.

Lord, thank you for using me despite myself. Thank you, Lord, for your power and glory that persists to move regardless of my human brokenness. Lord, may you never cease to wake me up from my repeated spiritual slumber, and may I never cease to stand in awe of your matchless grace and love that bring me back to you time and time again.

YOUR STORY

Read and reflect upon Luke 9:28–35. Then consider the following questions:

1. Was it wrong for Jesus's friends to fall asleep while he prayed? Was it understandable? Why or why not?

2. Try to put yourself in the place of the disciples. How do you think they felt about going up with Jesus when they were so tired? Do you think their feelings changed once they saw Jesus transfigured?

3. Now try to put yourself in the place of Jesus. How do you think he might have felt when they fell asleep? Was he frustrated, sad, understanding?

4. Can you think of a time when a situation or task that seemed mundane or inconvenient to you turned out to be a blessing?

5. Think about some of the everyday tasks that you may not enjoy doing (e.g., driving in traffic, laundry, unpleasant tasks at work). Think for a moment with the eyes of your imagination. How might the Lord use these everyday things to show God's glory to you, in you, and through you?

6. Think of some of the ways that the Lord has worked miracles in your life, or through you into the lives of others. This may include medical miracles, finding money in an unexpected place when you needed it, bringing someone into your life, or anything that demonstrated God's glory. Spend time in prayer, praising the Lord for these blessings.

CHAPTER 6

THE COUCH THAT DROPPED FROM HEAVEN
Sustaining Grace

God will meet all your needs according to the riches of his glory in
Christ Jesus.
Philippians 4:19

OUR STORY

"Lord, please bless me with physical hardship. Make it chronic and incurable."

"Jesus, if only I could have more bills than income, I just know then my life would be complete."

"God, send a few broken relationships my way, will ya? My family is just not dysfunctional enough."

I will surely never hear these prayers spoken aloud. First of all, it would take either severe masochism or extreme mental density for a person to ask for more troubles than life already provides. Even those who may feel such tendencies towards self-hurt would not dare publicly attest to such in a church prayer meeting.

Second, we do not generally look toward these sorts of human struggle as a source of great blessings and joy. In the midst of these struggles, we tend to look for God to pull us out of the mess, not to come sit next to us within it.

It may strike us as well and good to ride through a difficulty or two in life, as long as they are quick rides, or perhaps quick stops on the fast track to prosperity and success. Some of us (myself much included) find it quite frustrating when reminded that God does not always—does not usually—work that way. It does bring some comfort to know that God is patient with us works in progress. Too bad we do not always return the favor in confident expectation of the work God has in progress in our own lives.

Who could blame us for preferring the good, easy, and beautiful things in life? Who could blame us for wanting to get through the tough stuff as quickly as possible? God has, after all, created us to live life to the fullest (John 10:10), not the hungriest. Why would anyone pray to keep a thorn in the flesh?

Still, it helps to remember that God's idea of fullness and prosperity differs greatly from our own. As I reach so longingly for that grace that pulls me out of that pit of despair, it might help my own heart to recognize the powerful grace that can sustain and bless me in the midst of it all.

MY STORY

Our brief stay in California taught me a great deal about God's sustaining grace. When the job offer came through, I was ecstatic to hear that I would receive almost two and a half times my very modest salary. It did not worry me that unlike my current position, the California job would not come with furnished housing. Surely a 140% raise would cover the difference in rent, electricity, and utilities. And with a bigger job pool, we expected Ben to land better paying employment in no time.

When I arrived on the job in LA County, I soon found that due to an enormous misunderstanding between myself and human resources, along with my failure to confirm my understandings in writing, I would be receiving $10,000 (almost 20%) less a year than I had originally expected. Shock number two came a week later, when the risk management department informed me that the company through which I had transferred to this new position had different benefits packages in this new area. Consequently, it would cost almost $6,500 more (almost ten times as much) per year for my family's healthcare coverage.

Several other nickel-and-dime expenses augmented our fiscal stress. The grocery strike made food more expensive, gas prices spiked, and all of a sudden, we had to pay for parking everywhere we went. The final blow came when the cheapest decent living place we could find cost two to three times as much as a similar dwelling in our old area. This did not include utilities, laundry costs, or the expense to rent a refrigerator, none of which we paid at our previous apartment.

Those housing fees alone would have eaten up an entire month's pay in New York. Also, with the rising unemployment rate, it seemed impossible for my husband Ben to get a decent job, especially one that would pay for our infant's childcare expense. We ultimately ended up worse off financially—much worse off—in California than we had been before moving.

Two months after the move we sat in our small living room with boxes for our seats, a box for our table, and a box for our television stand. Boxes of books, albums, and mementos filled the living room. There was no point in unpacking them because we had nothing to fill the empty space. We couldn't even afford to buy the cheapest couch at a thrift store.

Times were tough. Nevertheless, the Lord also brought about great blessings in our lives through that California experience. One of our greatest blessings came through our close-knit church family there. One week during a meeting of our discipleship group, the pastor reminded us of Christ's promise in John 15:7, "If you remain in me and my words remain in you, ask whatever you wish, and it will be given you." He challenged us to bring our needs and desires to the Lord, and to lay them at God's feet.

In my heart, I took that promise to God. "Okay, Lord. You said that I could ask for what I wish. I want a couch." The Lord responded immediately and specifically. In my heart I perceived these words from God, "You want a couch? Fine. But you have to make space for it. I will give you a couch when the boxes get cleared out of the living room."

I had expected God to answer with a simple yes or no, by either giving us the couch or letting us go for a time without one. I did not expect to hear God's actual voice, or for the Lord to answer with such a clear and pointed message. I seriously questioned whether the voice came from the Lord or from my own thoughts.

That evening, when we got home, I shared my experience with Ben.

"Honey, I asked God for a couch tonight. And I'm not totally sure about this, but I think I got an answer."

"Oh, yeah? What did God say to you?"

"God told me that we will get our couch, but we have to do something first. We need to unpack the boxes and clean up the living room to make room for it."

The look on Ben's face in response to my story came as no surprise.

"Ben, you think I have lost my mind, don't you?"

"Pretty much."

I suspect that Ben thought that I was telling him this in order to encourage him to unpack all of the boxes. I was not sure that was not the case. I did not think it would hurt to clean up the living room, but Ben did not see any point in doing all that work just to have an empty space. I saw his point, and I myself did not look forward to helping him unpack, so I did not push the matter with him.

About six weeks later we still had no couch, and we couldn't take it anymore. So, we decided that over the weekend we would go thrift-store shopping and pray that God would provide us with at least enough money to buy something modest, having no idea from where the money might come.

On the next day, a Friday, Ben decided to surprise me by unpacking and cleaning the entire living room. I think the effort came in part from wishful thinking that the money for the couch would somehow drop from the sky. In reality, we knew that our Saturday furniture-seeking excursion would only involve window-shopping.

Before we left on Saturday morning, we found an unexpected blessing in the mail. After almost four months of our being in California, our old cable company from back in New York sent us a reimbursement check for $89.10. We thought that we could perhaps put this in the bank to start saving up enough money for some furniture.

As new residents in the area, we actually got lost on the way to the intended thrift store, and we ended up stumbling upon a cheaper one across town. One couch in particular from this store caught my eye. Just to humor myself, I took a peek at the price tag—$89. This was less than a third the price of a used sofa at the average thrift store where we had lived before. Finally, we had found one thing in California that was *less* expensive than other places! And thanks to the unexpected check, we found something we could actually afford.

Having forgotten about my earlier conversation with God, I did not at first make the connection between Ben's obedience and our furniture funding. Ben reminded me of this at the check-out counter. "Hey honey," he said casually, "I guess God really did speak to you a few weeks back."

"What do you mean?"

"You said that God told you that we would get a couch when we cleared out the living room. Well, we cleared out the living room, and the very next day we got a check for $89.10, almost the exact amount needed for our $89. couch, which we found 'by accident' for a really good price at a store where we never even intended to shop. That can't just be coincidence."

I smiled at God's sense of humor, and I marveled at the Lord's awesome ability to keep promises and meet our needs no matter what life's circumstance. Then, as I thought a bit more, I turned to my husband in only a partially playful scolding voice: "You mean to tell me I could have had a couch six weeks ago?"

GOD'S STORY

Our couch experience reminds me a little of the Israelites' plight after escaping from slavery in Egypt. At first, excitement and relief must have consumed them.

Not only had God just liberated them from the hands of their inhumane oppression and slavery in Egypt but the Lord's power and provision had enabled them to do the inconceivable. They walked right through a raging Red Sea without getting wet, straight to their freedom, and they defeated the world's strongest army without using a single earthly weapon.

Thus began their journey from slavery to the Promised Land of Canaan, their heritage from ancestors Abraham, Isaac, and Jacob. They were to take ownership of their own nation, free to enjoy all the fruits of their labor in a land flowing with milk and honey. God's blessings were theirs for the claiming, all within a short reach.

Their hearts must have been so full. However, the fullness in their hearts quickly yielded to the inevitable emptiness of their stomachs. In their mad dash from Egypt, they probably did not think much about the fact that they had so little to eat. In their anticipation of the prize, they failed to recognize the need for a journey—a challenging journey—through the dry wilderness.

Eventually the prospect of slavery and Egypt did not look quite so bad.

The pains of starvation led the Israelites to do one of the things that really, really hungry people sometimes do. They complained. "Moses, what were you thinking, promising us freedom only to bring us to our deaths of starvation? At least in Egypt we had our fill of food and drink. We'll be willing to go back and grovel for a good meal. Anything is better than this" (Exodus 16:2–3, author's paraphrase).

They would rather have gone back to the tyranny of whippings and ever-increasing, back-breaking oppression than to endure their hunger in the desert. Can anyone really blame them for reacting this way? They had achieved a level of comfort with their lot in life, a pattern to which they had grown accustomed. How could Moses be so cruel as to stir them all to the point of hope, only to bring them down even farther to the brink of utter despair and inevitable death?

They all knew the truth—that they could never go back to Egypt. After such a humiliating defeat of the Egyptian army at the Red Sea while the Israelites escaped, the Pharaoh would probably torture and humiliate them. Then he would either have them killed or make their life so unbearable that they would wish for death. Stuck in a desperate limbo, they could not go back, and they did not know how to go forward—not without fuel for the journey.

Then the miracle happened. Without their going on a single hunt or planting a single seed, pastries and delicacies began appearing before their very eyes. Each morning's dew brought with it a light and flaky pastry. They had never seen anything like it, so they called it manna (which literally means "what is it?"). And forget about raining cats and dogs. It rained quail, a gourmet-style poultry. Not only did God feed them . . . the Lord fed them with style.

Had the Israelites shown faith in God's promise, this quail and manna would have served as only a temporary meal plan on their short journey to Canaan. But their unbelief, mistakes, and disobedience led to forty years of sinful wandering through the Desert of Sin. (Really, that is its name.) Nevertheless, God never ceased to meet their needs. As a result, their children met their destinies in the Promised Land with full stomachs.

Ben and I left for California with expectations of quickly reaching our own Promised Land. Financially speaking, it seemed a lot more like the Desert of Sin, leaving us worse off monetarily than we had ever been, with no prospects of going back to where we had been. Nevertheless, God always met our needs, teaching us valuable lessons about trust and obedience along the way.

The couch was not the only thing that seemed to drop from Heaven during that time. Within weeks the Lord sent us the rest of the furniture we needed for our home. He also sent us an amazing small group of people who met on that very furniture weekly for the next year and a half as a prayer and support group, all of whom still hold a place very dear to our hearts.

Lord, thank you for always meeting my needs, for sustaining me even in life's driest seasons. In those times in which I seem parched and thirsty for hope, please help me to look up, and to wait expectantly for the blessing that you will rain down upon me, as you always do.

YOUR STORY

Read and reflect upon Exodus 16. Then consider the following questions:

1. Did the Israelites have a right to panic and complain? Why or why not?

2. Egypt was a place of slavery, oppression, and hurt for the Israelites. Have you ever had an Egypt in your life, a bad circumstance beyond your control from which you needed freedom? Is this true of your life now?

3. Can you think of a time when God's grace sustained you while you were dealing with a rough situation? Explain.

4. The Wilderness of Sin was that dry, monotonous, difficult place that the Israelites wandered around in, on their way to the Promised Land. Since all Christians are works in progress, we all experience some sort of wilderness difficulties on our journey between the sinful life and Heaven. What is your wilderness? Have you ever felt like you stepped out in faith, only for God to leave you hanging? Have you ever considered turning back to Egypt over the hard journey toward Jesus?

5. What sorts of things keep you in your wilderness experience? Are there any factors that you can control or change? Can you recognize any ways in which the Lord is sustaining you in the process?

CHAPTER 7

Confessions of an Unforgiving Servant

Forgiving Grace - The House, Part 1

Forgive, and you will be forgiven.
Luke 6:37

OUR STORY

In today's economy, it seems difficult for many of us not to have a torrid love affair with our credit card companies. We love to use the plastic. They in turn love to charge us repeated, compounding interest on our purchases. With so much credit available to the average consumer, and with so many projects and needs around our household, it almost seems impossible not to use these extensions of money, money we do not own.

In the face of certain tragedy or loss, it may in fact be impossible to refrain from leaning upon the long arm of credit. The difficulties come when we choose (or are forced) to lean so heavily on debt-producing means that we scarcely have the ability to stand on our own two feet.

Some wise, discerning, and blessed individuals (myself not included) have managed to steer clear of the trap of debt altogether. By the grace of God, others manage to pull little by little out of the hole, though slower than we would like. Still others just drown in that great sea of bills and creditors.

This truth reaches beyond just financial issues. Life calls upon us to juggle many priorities and projects, and I for one am no juggler. In order to hold on to some things, we have to let other things go, and I do not always find it so easy to choose. Sometimes my body seems to choose what my mind does not want.

Do I want to hold on to my habit of sleeping in and let my body fall into lower levels of fitness? Not really, except when I hear the alarm clock in the morning. Do I want to let go of my habit of eating out so much and hold onto the idea of paying off debt? Absolutely, until I get hungry and tired after a long day's work.

This is not always all a matter of fault. I work really hard and have a family that needs me, along with a lot of other projects. Sometimes I just need to let my hair down and rest, but how do I do so without letting my whole self go? Does this sound familiar to anyone out there?

When we choose wrongly or incorrectly, or even when forces beyond our control leave us without a healthier choice, we can end up with some sort of deficit, whether financial, physical, emotional, or spiritual. This creates opportunities for indebtedness to others. In the best of cases, we feel eternal gratitude toward those who help us out in ways that we can never repay. In the worst of times, we sometimes cause irrevocable damage, hurting people in ways for which we can never make up.

Whether it be a matter of fault or circumstance (the two are not mutually exclusive), life can really get us in a rut. Understanding this helps me to show grace and forgiveness to the other tired, worn-out, debt-laden men and women out there. That said, I easily forget.

MY STORY

My husband Ben and I bought our first home at the peak of a booming housing market. Property values had doubled and, in some cases, tripled in many areas of town within a three-year period. We tended to browse through the local real-estate magazines with wide eyes, continually shocked at the value placed on even the most modest of properties. As we mused about the proverbial dream home we would like to purchase someday, a more practical side of me began to think that owning any sort of a home may only happen in our dreams.

When I first saw the little grayish-blue home with the picket fence, I thought to myself, "Oh, how cute." Then my eyes moved to a curious sight, one less digit in the price than the others. This house advertised for a third of the average listing we read in the real-estate magazines. Once this detail caught my eye, I had another thought. "We could actually afford this one."

I pointed out the advertisement to Ben, and we called the realtor to make an inquiry. The small but adequate house—a nine-hundred-square-foot, two-bedroom bungalow—could easily accommodate our young family of three. Once we discovered the neighborhood in which it was located, we weren't so sure that we wanted to be there for long. We thought we may even just keep it as an income-making rental property. But it was a house, a steppingstone to better living, and the professional home inspector whom we hired to check the place out reported it to be in quite good condition for its age.

Our realtor recommended an incredible loan officer who found us a better than average rate for first-time homeowners who planned to occupy the purchased property, should we care to buy. At this rate, we would actually pay hundreds of dollars less a month on our mortgage than we spent on rent for the townhome in which we lived at the time.

One thing led to another, and before we knew it, we were signing the final paperwork at the property lawyer's office. We marveled at just how easy and inexpensive the whole home-buying process had been. The seller had made enough monetary concessions that we needed to bring less than ten dollars to the table for closing costs.

We even inherited an "excellent renter," (or so the realtor told us) who was contracted to pay us about $250 more than the scheduled mortgage payment each month. If we so chose, we would be able to move into the home when her lease ended nine months later. Or we could ride the wave of income-bearing home ownership. The situation could not have been more perfect.

Then came the end of the month, and the due date for the rent payment from our excellent renter. When at first she did not deliver our money on time, we saw no point in acting heavy handed. We wanted to avoid any sort of dissension or ill relations, if possible. I figured that perhaps we had not communicated with her well enough concerning where to send the check. I sent her a quick note and left a message on her cell phone to clarify matters.

Another week passed, and she still failed to contact us. I gave her another call and left her another message. She finally called back. At first, she seemed remorseful for avoiding us and eager to work towards paying us. She told us that she was trying to work with the department of social services to get help with paying the rent. She vowed that if we met with her and signed some paperwork, they would help her catch up on her rent right away.

A most frustrating fifteen days followed. Within days of that promise her phone service got disconnected. The tenant also failed to return any of our letters or respond to house visits. We later found out that this excellent renter had not even paid her rent to the previous landlord for three months. From the looks of the other notices posted on her door and in the house, she also fell months behind on about every other bill.

Though highly perturbed, our understanding of her situation led us to feel a bit of compassion for her. A single parent of three children, she had moved out of her mother's house in her first true attempt at financial independence. The combined incomes of her and her co-renter fiancé (whom we originally thought was her husband) was enough to cover the bills, until the cops discovered the source of her fiancé's income.

Her fiancé's inevitable arrest for drug possession left her with all of the bills. Then she somehow lost her own temporary-to-hire position. Things seemed to spiral out of control for her from there.

As Christians, we did not feel this situation merited our harsh judgment or callous demands. After some prayer on the matter, we resolved to give her the opportunity to get out of the lease without any legal repercussions. We even decided not to hold her responsible for the six weeks of rent she already owed us, and we gave her two full weeks to finish packing and move. All she had to do was leave the place in good condition.

Now if we could only get in touch with her to let her know this.

I so wanted to reach out to this woman and let her know that she did not have to be afraid of us. Even more, I wanted her to at least acknowledge our existence. Her blatant evasion of us quickly changed my attitude.

Though Ben maintained the resolution to forgive the woman at all costs, I took a different road. Along with her first eviction notice, I sent her a strongly worded letter giving her the ultimatum to either contact us or go to court for the remainder of the rent, which was a several-thousand-dollar amount and could lead to garnishment of her wages. I felt only a small willingness to show this woman grace, as long as the grace came on my terms.

Eventually she called and said she would be out of the house with everything cleaned immaculately in a week. She would leave the key when she finished cleaning. Three weeks later her furniture had vanished, but she left behind a huge mess, complete with enough garbage to fill and overflow a supersized dumpster. We could not even get to some parts of the house without climbing over a mountain of broken toys and old clothes, along with a pile of brand-new, name-brand men's clothing with the tags still on them. She never did return the key.

She had also left food in the refrigerator, though the electricity had been turned off more than a month earlier. To add insult to injury, the woman left a utilized training toilet in the house. When the training toilet filled up, she had dumped it on our living room carpet several times! The southern summer heat, along with a refrigerator full of perishables, or rather fully perished food, further augmented the unbearable sight and smell.

For a time, we could not even walk into the house without wearing masks. Her complete lack of regard had turned our little dream into a nightmare. We could not even claim a tax deduction on the thousands and thousands of dollars of repair that her negligence had caused. Since she never paid us a dime in rent, we could not list the repair as a cost of business.

I was furious! I would have helped that woman any way she asked. I even would have helped her clean her house. We kept giving her grace over and over again, only to have our faces spit upon by her ingratitude and disregard.

At this point I went for the jugular. Obviously, the renter did not want our help, nor did she care at all about us. I appointed myself as the one to teach her a lesson about grace. I wanted to show her that if she was not willing to accept my repeated offers of grace, and on my terms, then she deserved whatever she got from me. In retrospect, it did not make a very good lesson for either of us.

This reasonable little voice in my head kept telling me the most sensible things. "You have to sue her, so she doesn't do this to anyone else." "Who cares if she has small children? She's probably living with her mother now, and someone else is paying her bills." "Obviously God has sent you to teach her a lesson about responsibility, so help her be responsible by holding her accountable in court."

It absolutely amazes me how convincingly Satan can disguise his voice as the voice of reason. And yet, as I resolved to do all these things—to sue, to garnish wages, to blemish her credit, *to give her what she deserved*—I felt an increasing burden of negativity well up within me as my sense of peace departed. I cannot count the number of sleepless nights and tears shed in anger, disgust, and hurt.

I remember complaining to God one day about this despicable woman. I said "Lord, I just wanted to help her. I wanted to show her grace, and give her a free gift, and all she keeps doing is ignoring me, and spitting in the face of my help."

In a message that could only come from God, my Lord replied with six of the most difficult words I have ever heard. "How do you think I feel?"

Ouch!

With that statement, God put me in the same boat as that ungrateful renter. How could I possibly judge someone just like me?

For months I had been asking the Lord what I should do with the renter. This time I stopped ignoring the answer I kept hearing. "Karen, you know what you need to do. Forgive this woman. Release her from her debt to you."

"But Lord, she has wronged me so very much. She has multiplied wrong upon wrong. How could you possibly let her get away with this?"

"Karen, this is not about her. This is about you and me. Forgive her and trust me to meet your needs." I later realized that I could not even enjoy the fullness of freedom and forgiveness God offered me until I fully forgave her, with no strings attached.

Here's the kicker, something I had known deep down all along. In the end, I was the one responsible for my rental situation, because in the beginning I chose to assent to a little white lie (there is no such thing, by the way) over trusting God to meet my needs. I wanted to receive the special interest rate loan that enabled us to afford the property. In order to secure it, I initialed a statement saying that we planned to move into the house within ninety days, though I knew full well that the lease lasted at least another nine months.

It was one of about thirty short statements that I needed to initial on the loan document, so I reasoned that I was telling the truth everywhere else, I would pay the mortgage every month, and eventually we *might* live in the house for a bit, some day. So, I and I alone initialed the statement saying that we would occupy the house within three months, reasoning that it was just a tiny discrepancy among pages of initialed promises that were 100 percent accurate. I had justified the fraud, lying even to myself that God was okay with it, because it would help us get ahead.

Ironically, telling the truth would have protected me from years of heartache and inconvenience, and tens of thousands of dollars of expense. Ironically, that renter's dishonesty forced me to follow through on that commitment to occupy that home we bought. With all of the money she cost us, and the damage to the property, we could not afford to live anywhere else.

As a person who prides myself on living with the highest degree of integrity, it took me a while to come to terms with the truth that I had willingly chosen to violate my own standards and, more importantly, break God's law. The rope of righteousness that unites us with God gets just as broken and unusable with one snip, one little white lie (and trust me, I've sinned more than that) as it does when someone slashes it repeatedly on a daily basis. Laying aside all the other ways I've sinned throughout my life, that one lie alone left me in the same place as the renter, wherever she may be—broken and badly in need of God's grace.

I struggled with animosity and judgment of the renter for weeks, each day feeling greater anger and less peace. As I finally surrendered to God's call to forgive, I felt my peace restored. I approached Ben the next day about forgiving our tenant of all rent and damages. He readily agreed, noting that he had only been waiting and praying for my agreement to do so all along.

In response, the Lord both met our needs and replaced my mourning with joy. We paid off the additional debt she caused us within a year, and the experience itself inspired me to begin writing, which led to a great deal of healing in my own heart.

I soon noticed another irony of it all. The more I tried to hold onto control and to take back what I felt was mine, the more I lost myself. When I finally let go of my need to get even, God provided both the peace and the monetary provision that I had sought from the beginning.

GOD'S STORY

In the parable of the unforgiving servant, found in Matthew 18:21–35, a servant owed a king an amount equal to about ten thousand times what an average worker would make in his entire lifetime. Given the average US household income, this would equal roughly ten billion dollars nowadays.

This very figure shows evidence of the servant's recklessness and disregard with money. A smaller amount of debt might reasonably incur through medical expenses, basic needs, or a bout of misfortune. But to spend ten thousand lifetimes of money actually takes work. This leads me to wonder what on earth could have led this man to exhibit such exceedingly reckless disregard.

Conceivably, vanity may have led him to try keeping up a certain appearance of wealth that he simply did not have. Maybe he had gambling issues. Perhaps a felt loneliness led him to hire professional companionship of a most unholy sort. More likely than not, this kind of debt involved any combination of vices.

Whatever the reason, it probably involved some sort of addiction that drove him to keep compulsively spending money that did not even belong to him. One might also infer that this foolish servant nurtured the irrational hope that the king would never notice that much money missing, for he could never have paid this amount back.

When caught, the servant stood before the king and made a most desperate promise. Facing nothing less than a lifetime of imprisonment, he told the king that if given time, he would pay the entire amount back. Both he and the king must have recognized the impossibility, the sheer absurdity of this prediction. The servant would have said anything, grasped at any straw in a situation fraught with imminent punishment that he knew he could not escape.

The king's response defied belief. Faced with an enormous loss from the royal treasury, this great and loving ruler wiped the servant's slate clean, as if he owed the king nothing at all. He did not punish the servant. He did not put the servant on a payment plan. He did not even reduce the debt. He just forgave.

One might think that the servant would remember the king's grace to him, a lowly subject. Yet no sooner had the king set him free, than he sent his own friend to prison over an amount that was equal to about one hundred days' pay. A third of a year's wages seems enormous at first. But when contrasted with the amount owed to the king, it is next to nothing. The hypocrisy in this circumstance turns my stomach.

Comparison of this parable in light of our rental situation really hit home for me. When you add up the missed rent, damage to the house, and fees that our tenant cost us, she owed us almost exactly one hundred days' wages. To be sure, this cost enough to put a real strain on our household finances. Yet in comparison to the infinite debt that I owe my heavenly king, it equals virtually nothing.

How many times have I knowingly and willingly denied and ignored God, adding yet more to the debt that I already cannot pay? How many times do I promise to make it up to God, never to do it again, only to fall flat on my face?

Yet my great and loving king continually wipes my slate clean, as if I owed the Lord nothing at all. God does not usually punish me, at least not to the extent that I deserve. God does not put me on a payment plan. God does not even reduce the debt. God simply forgives. Hallelujah, Jesus already paid my debt!

I have discovered that true forgiveness has so very little to do with the other person. I never met that renter face to face. But who *she* was, good or bad, did not matter, beyond that fact that she was—and IS—a child for whom Christ died. What always matters most is who God is and who I choose to be in Christ.

We can trust God to take care of those who harm us. In the meantime, we can trust God to take care of us and remove the burden of judgment that would otherwise forfeit our healing and erode our spirit. But just like the servant in this parable, we have got to be willing to forgive the lesser debts owed to us by others in order to unlock the infinite grace that God will freely give us. We cannot at the same time have our fists closed by hanging on to offense and judgment and opened to receive God's blessing.

True forgiveness in the face of real hurt can be a difficult process that costs us dearly. A hundred days of wages is no joke. And yet, when we look at the benefits—the infinitely greater forgiveness we receive from God, the freedom from that satanic foothold that our judgment creates, and the right to our full inheritance as children of God—well, the choice should be clear.

It has become clear to me that between the tenant and myself, I know that I have been forgiven the greater debt by far.

Lord, forgive my hypocritical double standard. May I not soon forget your generosity, that forgives all no matter what the cost. May I remember my eternal indebtedness to you and echo such grace when faced with those who cannot pay their earthly bills. And when I do forget, when I do judge others, unwilling to withdraw my self-righteous judgment, please draw me close, lovingly convict me, and forgive me yet again.

YOUR STORY

Read and Reflect upon Matthew 18:15–35. Then consider and discuss the following:

1. Find yourself in this story. With what character can you most closely identify? Can you identify with more than one character?

2. Do you trust God enough to completely forgive everyone who has harmed you? Do you trust God to take care of your needs? Do you trust God to justly handle the person who harmed you?

3. **List 1:** List the people and things in your life that have hurt you severely, whether financially, emotionally, or otherwise. Next, list people or things over the past month who have offended, annoyed, or angered you, even in the smallest way. (Like the driver who cut you off last week.)

4. **List 2:** Ask the Lord to reveal to you any major way that you have offended, angered, or hurt God: over your lifetime, the past year, or even just the past couple of days (e.g., an impure thought, a critical or judgmental attitude, hateful attitudes towards others, etc.). Write it down. Give yourself some time. These two lists could take a while.

5. Look at list 2. Christians, for those of which you have already repented, know that God has forgiven you. Lay the rest at God's feet and ask forgiveness. If you have not yet accepted Jesus Christ as your Savior, consider doing so now. It is as easy as a, b, c: **a**dmitting your need for help and grace from God; **b**elieving that Jesus is your Lord, God, and Savior; and **c**ommitting to live your life for God. This is not about flawlessness. It's about facing your heart in the right direction.

6. Know that there is "no condemnation for those who are in Christ Jesus" (Romans 8:1), and praise God for the Lord's infinite grace. If necessary, forgive yourself, for this is the command of the Lord. Be sure to leave your sins at Jesus's feet before going to the next step.

7. Return to list 1. Think of what total forgiveness of all these people, organizations, and things would cost you. Then think of what total forgiveness of your sins cost Christ. (Christ's comfort, Christ's status, Christ's very life.) Meditate on the following statement: God only asks us to forgive as much as we want God to forgive us. In fact, if we were to add up the offenses of everything and everyone throughout our entire lives, that could not even approach the debt that we owe God.

8. Cross out those on your list whom you have already forgiven. Then look through the rest and pray for the strength to release them from your judgment. Forgive those whom you can forgive, committing them to God. Be honest. If there are those whom you cannot bring yourself to forgive right now, write their names on a clean sheet, and carry them around in your Bible. Pray for them and yourself every day until the Lord grants you the strength to let go of their debt.

CHAPTER 8

THE BARK THAT BROKE THE CAMEL'S BACK
Struggling Grace

For our struggle is not against flesh and blood.
Ephesians 6:12

OUR STORY

"Okay, you two, I want to see a good, clean fight." The classic opening mantra of a boxing referee. The ref says this in promotion of the idea that in order to fight well, one must also fight fairly. It doesn't hurt that a good, clean fight makes the referee's job for the match much easier.

That kind of logic is all well and good in the ring; but in real life doesn't that term "a good, clean fight" seem like a bit of an oxymoron? Does not the very idea of fighting bring with it the connotation that at least one of the parties has failed to act in a good or clean manner?

In order to even touch this issue in a logical manner, we must first ask what it really means to fight. As with the first question, the answer depends entirely on one's perspective.

We often tend to visualize the negative interpretations of fighting. The comic-book version casts a character of ultimate good against evil. One wins such a struggle by battering and bruising the loser, amidst the screams and cheers of the on-looking crowd. In the schoolyard version, either the bad guy bully ends up beating up on a poor victim, or two bad eggs who cannot hold their temper fight one another.

In another, perhaps purer sense, fighting means struggling, either for or against something. By this standard, fighting need not always involve violence or negative attitudes. Civil rights icon Martin Luther King fought effectively against racial inequality without ever lifting a fist. More commonly, our country currently houses many recovering addicts fighting to stay clean, young men and women fighting to keep their bodies sexually pure, struggling couples fighting to keep the love in their marriage alive, and countless others striving to move forward. Who would argue against the validity of such wars?

The struggle itself does not fully define the nature of the fight. One might fight for the right things but do so in the wrong ways. Some people fight to save unborn children—a worthy cause—by attacking the already confused and tormented women who enter the clinics, seeking to fight against sin by attacking the sinner. Cutting, anorexia, and other forms of masochism draw people to battle their problems by inflicting pain upon themselves. Some try to fight passive-aggressiveness by either ignoring or evading problems. These misguided solutions only further aggravate the situation.

To fight in the *wrong* way may actually produce the very result a person has feared. Many parents fight to produce disciplined children by exhibiting controlling, punitive, and overbearing attitudes. This sometimes ends up pushing their kids to a level of rebellion that far exceeds their parents' grasp. Others fight to feel loved and accepted by compromising their morals and values to fit in with others; in the end this generally leaves them feeling even greater degrees of self-hatred and unacceptability.

So, what exactly defines the difference between a dirty battle and a good, clean fight? Perhaps that is all a matter of choosing our battles, weapons, and methods wisely. It also sometimes involves an understanding of our motives for fighting in the first place.

MY STORY

My marriage has provided the most natural arena in which to work out the logistics of healthy and unhealthy struggle. The reality of our deep mutual love compels us to work daily toward better communication and more respectful conflict resolution. The reality that Ben possesses the singularly unique ability to get on every last nerve in my body, and undoubtedly vice versa, often makes the task difficult for both of us.

I know how to hold my temper, and I can generally keep my cool around just about anyone. Ben, however, has this supernatural ability to severely aggravate me without even saying a word. He easily pushes those buttons which lay hidden to the rest of the world. Sometimes he strikes me as a master musician, able to skillfully play up and down the keyboard of my emotions, sometimes for nothing more than his own general amusement.

He usually need not even speak to get me going. A slight raise of the eyebrow or movement of the hand at the right moment can work wonders to ignite my fire. I do not know how he does it. I often feel like a puppet in his hands.

Sometimes he pretends to act serious about certain things only to laugh at me when I get all flustered. Other times he comes openly in jest. He will interrupt me with some sort of nonsense while I try to focus on work or something else important to me. He will work all of those nerves he knows so well.

Then finally, when my carefully guarded composure explodes with some sour face or nasty comment, he'll just smile at me with that annoyingly loving smile (well, it's annoying at that point at least) and say something like "You're so cute." Then he might give me a kiss or hug. So, I do not even get the satisfaction of staying angry with him over it all.

This only describes the playful button-pushing. When in arguments, his pushing and prodding can lead to not-so-silly results. When I allow him to really, seriously work me up, I can occasionally abandon the restraint of which I might otherwise boast.

During the early years of our marriage, before we learned how to fight more fairly, our periodic arguments led me to do some pretty wild things. I said many a word that I would not otherwise say. I threw things—most notably a spike-heeled shoe—at his head. (I purposely missed, but he caught the sentiment.) I even locked him out of the house a couple of times.

Once I went so far as to try and take up smoking, which I have always hated with a passion, just to get back at him. Fortunately, I had no idea how to light a cigarette properly. By the time I figured it out, I had broken down in tears too heavily to take a puff.

God has worked with me on this. I no longer fly off the handle quite so easily or severely with him. However, on the rare occasions that we do work ourselves up into a good fight, well let's just say that I am still not so nice to him in these circumstances. I suppose it would not be a fight, or at least not for very long, if only one of us acted ugly.

Strangely enough, our fighting usually doesn't seem to be about the big stuff. We both possess a marked fear about messing up the course of our lives that leads us to take the weightier concerns to God. This sort of paranoia has actually served us rather well. When we disagree about a major issue, we usually pray about it and ask the Lord to give us direction and peace about the right answer.

Our most heated disagreements have almost always resulted from the smaller issues. I couldn't count the number of times that we fought over who would change Ali's diaper when she was a baby. Those little tiffs generally took exponentially longer amounts of time and energy than just changing her diaper in the first place.

We have also co-participated in some knock-down, drag-out disagreements over matters of money as small as five dollars, or over whom to blame when the laundry piled up. The term "the straw that broke the camel's back" applies rather well to such situations. Just like that one tiny, almost weightless amount that pushed the camel beyond its loading capacity, these sorts of quarrels often result from those tiniest "straws" of life that effectively push us each beyond our own limits.

One such brawl involved the question of who should get up a couple of minutes early that morning to take our new dog Spot outside. It may not seem like much now, but at the time it turned out to be the bark that broke the camel's back.

Within the previous two months' time, a few major things had happened. First, we found and adopted a puppy, a beautiful, high-maintenance mutt, which brought our family both measureless joy and endless headaches.

Second, our daughter Ali graduated from preschool. We took her out of day care for the summer, to both save money for her private-school tuition in the fall and to give me more time to spend with her before she began kindergarten. This put a lot of extra stress on me, as I now faced the challenge of how to both work full-time from home and entertain a five-year-old all day long. On top of this, I had to stay up late to complete some other freelance projects to which I had committed.

Finally, Ben found a few serious issues with the house, and by a few, I mean we had pieces of the bathroom and kitchen scattered throughout our home and yard. This put much extra stress on him, as he struggled with his own juggling act between work and trying to fix the house. At the same time, Ben was trying to fulfill some promises he had made to help out various friends of ours from church.

Meanwhile, we had this relentless little yapper in our home intent on stealing away any hope either of us had of even a moment's peace. He would scream out for attention throughout the day, constantly distracting me from my work.

No matter how much I stopped to pay him attention, it was never enough. No matter where I put him, inside or outside, the backyard or the front yard, he always barked and whined to be somewhere else. He never stopped. It did not matter whether he felt happy or sad, needy or satisfied. He just yelped away to the full extent of his little doggy lungs. Were it not for the fact that our plumbing system already needed a total overhaul at that point, I may have tried to flush the dog down the toilet.

The fact that I never really wanted a dog to begin with further frustrated me. I told Ben that I was okay getting one as long as he and Ali took care of it. However, since Ben worked away from home, I was left to deal with the dog during the day.

The dog never seemed to sleep either. At night he would wake Ben up every hour on the hour. If Ben did not get up and take him outside, he would make a mess in his cage. The little mutt would continue to bark relentlessly throughout the night until Ben surrendered to his canine will. Spot wore me out so much during the day that I slept oblivious to the midnight howling, but Ben didn't.

One morning after a week or two of this constant schedule, Spot barked enough to wake me up at 5:45 a.m. This came during my last precious thirty minutes of allotted sleep that morning. I tried to wake up Ben, unaware that Spot had already gotten him up about five times throughout the night. Then came the fateful question from Ben, to the background tune of Spot's piercing squeals, "Honey, can you take Spot out for me this morning?"

I flipped out. I could not believe his audacity, knowing that I watched both Ali and the dog all day long, even after saying that I did not want to have to ever take care of the dog. He angrily pointed out that he had to spend a lot of extra time fixing all the stuff in the house, which left him exhausted. Not caring at all about this at the time, I flippantly said, "So what? You don't need this dog. We need these house repairs."

Had he no idea how worn out this all made me? Had he no idea what things I had to give up in order to be with both our daughter and the dog 24/7? I saw great value in doing so with Alethea, no matter how much she wore me out. The mutt, on the other hand. . . .

I calmly put on my shoes and announced that I would take the dog out—to the car—and on a nice trip across town—to the SPCA animal shelter. If Ben could not take care of him, I did not want to keep the puppy, no matter how cute he was. This led to the exchange of some other not-so-nice words. There was no talking sense into either one of us. By this point Ali had awakened and had caught wind of the fact that we might be giving her beloved puppy and only house companion away.

She started crying. I started crying. Ben stood amidst us, with this look in his eye of bewilderment. How has such a small issue led to such a big blow-up?

The release of my tears brought about a certain parallel flow of truth from my mouth. "Honey, I'm just so tired. I hear that dog barking all day long, and no matter what I do, it won't stop. I'm already feeling overwhelmed trying to work full-time, meet Ali's needs, make up for the fact that her daddy is working too hard on the house to see her enough, *and* I'm trying to do the freelance work at night. Taking out that dog once in the morning may not seem like a lot, but I'm already stretched beyond my limits, and I literally do not feel like I can do one more thing without breaking down."

Ben's tone softened. "I'm sorry, honey. I had no idea. I've been so overwhelmed myself. I have these stressful projects at work. I've had to fulfill these promises to help other people. And these housing issues are way more difficult and expensive to fix than I thought. I need to fix everything so that you and Ali have everything you need, and I'm not doing it quickly enough. On top of that, Spot gets me up once an hour throughout the entire night. I haven't had a decent night's sleep in over a week, and I'm always working."

"Spot's been getting you up that much? I didn't hear him."

"I know. I've been taking care of it to let you sleep." I felt horrible that I would so quickly attack this man who went beyond his limitations to try and meet my needs. I think he felt the same about me at that point.

With these new understandings, we quickly addressed the issue in a way that would satisfy both of us. We simply moved our rapidly growing dog to his new home under a shady tree in the backyard. Spot lived quite comfortably in the mild outdoor climate. Alethea could still play with him some during the day, which would both give her exercise and keep her occupied during some of the time I worked. With the move, the barking diminished from a constant stream of howls to the occasional cry for attention.

I suppose that, as with most of our disagreements, the fight became fair when we could identify the true conflict. In the beginning, each one of us mistook the other for the enemy, and we fought accordingly. In that sense, through our mutual attacks, we enabled a self-perpetuating problem. Realizing how many challenges the other faced enabled us to rejoin forces with one another and address our challenges on a united front.

Ben and I have yet to fully perfect this art of fighting well, which includes a fair and loving struggle toward resolution and mutual understanding. Sometimes it takes a few rounds, with a break or two in between, as we go to our separate corners of the house. Sometimes it involves unnecessary yelling. It almost always ends in apologies.

More and more often we will surrender our harsh tones in exchange for calm, determined conversation that continues to the point of mutual understanding and affirmation. Then, when we finally get it, we can move on without remorse, guilt, or any sort of anger at one another. I suspect that our arguing in some form will never end. But neither will our love and desire to always work things out.

GOD'S STORY

Jacob brought a lifetime of fighting experience to his great wrestling match with the Lord. It began with his birth. He earned his name, which means "he grasps at the heal" in Hebrew, by clinging to his brother Esau's foot on the way out of their mother's womb. This launched a decades-long campaign through which Jacob grasped at the rights and blessings of his older twin.

Jacob tended to win the struggles he waged against others, partly because he fought dirty. Always the opportunist, he refused to feed his brother, who stood before him at the point of starvation, until Esau agreed to sell his birthright for the bargain price of a bowl of soup. Having inherited his mother Rebekah's gene for deception, he (Rebekah's favorite child) worked with her to win himself Esau's paternal blessing. In order to do so, he exploited his own dying father's blindness and failing senses.

Once he conned Esau out of everything he held dear, Jacob found a reason to leave town. He used that excuse that he needed to travel to the place where Rebekah had grown up in order to find a wife. This left the older brother to care for and eventually bury their dying parents, without receiving any of the benefits that should have come with the responsibility.

When he reached his mother's homeland, Jacob finally experienced what it felt like to be on the receiving end of injustice. Uncle Laban, who also seemed to have inherited the deceptive gene, conned him into twenty years of service with little to no material gain to show for it. Still Jacob eventually won the upper hand, beating Laban at his own game. In doing so he seriously depleted Laban's fortune. Then once again Jacob left town, going back to his father's land, and leaving Laban to pick up the pieces.

As Jacob approached his homeland, and his brother whom he had cheated more than once, his web of deception came full circle. A head-on confrontation with his approaching twin seemed inevitable. He hoped that a heart-felt apology and a few fortune's worth of gifts could buy his forgiveness and safety. He further put off the inevitable by sending every item, animal, and person in his possession as a buffer between himself and his brother.

After sending his family, servants, and belongings over the last tributary that stood between Esau and himself, Jacob stayed back one more night. Perhaps he sought inner peace there. Instead, he met a very real outward attack. The Bible says, "A man wrestled with him till daybreak" (Genesis 32:24).

On that night, as Jacob prepared to face the music with his dejected brother, God taught him a new way to fight.

Here we see a new face to his character of persistent struggle. Previously Jacob seemed to win out over others almost too easily, through cunning and deception. This time he had to work for it, painfully and honestly. He had to give it his all. He did so for hours, and he walked away with a serious limp to prove it.

Who knows why Jacob wrestled so relentlessly with the stranger? He did not even know at the time that he struggled with the Lord. So he could not imagine the immense payoff his audacious persistence would bring. Was he that set on winning every game at all costs?

Perhaps Jacob simply sensed how important this struggle was, though he knew not why. Perhaps Jacob did not think at all. Life sometimes presents us all with those circumstances wherein fighting persistence, a refusal to give in all come as second nature. In those times we continue to "fight the good fight" without even considering alternatives.

Whatever the reason, Jacob would not give in. As a result, he gained a new name, along with a new way of life. Jacob, the heal grasper, became Israel, the man who "struggles with God." That night he changed from a man who always grabbed for what belonged to others into a man who reached for that which God had longed to give him all along.

As I reflect upon Israel, I again think about my Ben. What defines our struggle? Do we fight more against each other, trying to self-vindicate at the other's expense? Or do we fight together, against those forces that keep us from experiencing the fullness of God's grace in our lives? Truthfully, we do a little of both, but oh do I love those days when we get it right. Then the fight becomes an adventure, a battle well worth waging.

So, all in all, that concept of a good, clean fight works pretty well for us. Still, nowadays we try to keep our shoes in the closet in times of frustration—just in case.

Lord, thank you for all of the wonderful relationships with which you have blessed me. Forgive me for all of those times I let those petty differences get in the way of the loving interaction you long for me to share with others. Forgive me for those times I let my pride and selfishness get in the way of my relationship with you. Lord, bless my relationships.

May our continual struggle not be one of "flesh and blood" against one another, but rather a united battle for the right. May I live more in tune with your Holy Spirit, knowing when and how to fight only those battles you would have me fight, using only those weapons that You would provide.

YOUR STORY

Read and reflect upon Genesis 32:22–32. Then consider the following questions:

1. What kinds of struggles had Jacob waged against others in his lifetime?

2. How was Jacob's struggle with God (on the night before he met Esau) different than the other fights and disagreements he had with others?

3. What came of Jacob's struggle with the "mystery man"? How did it change him?

4. Can you think of a time when you had a fight or disagreement that led to disastrous results? Can you think of a time when you had a fight or conflict that led to an improvement in your life or situation?

5. How can you tell whether or not something is worth fighting for? How do you know whether or not you are fighting for it in the right way?

6. How do you deal with conflict in your life? Do you ignore it? Talk it out? Internalize it? Lash out? Do you feel you generally deal with conflict in healthy ways? How could you improve on your style of resolving conflict?

CHAPTER 9

THE WALMART CONVICTION
Sovereign Grace

My grace is sufficient for you, for my power is made perfect in weakness.
2 Corinthians 12:9

OUR STORY

Living by faith seems much simpler when life is easy. How could we deny God's grace and existence in our lives when we have money in the bank, little to no debt, ideal jobs, a full bill of health and fitness, community standing, and relationships that do not suffer any sort of dysfunction or drama?

(By the way, if you happen to ever meet someone like this, please give them my number. I would love to know their secret. I suspect that even those whose lives seem that perfect have their own struggles that they do not necessarily share with the outside world.)

Then again, without a little challenge here and there, the "comfortable faith" with which so many people live can quickly and easily erode into complacency and spiritual dryness. I question whether *comfortable* faith is faith at all.

Satan has plagued our nation with these spiritual forces of complacency and the illusion of control. For one thing, if we feel like we have everything we could possibly need on this earth, like we have our lives under control, then why would we have any reason to trust in God to meet our needs?

When we think we have everything together for ourselves, and when we become numb to the brokenness in ourselves and those around us, we often simultaneously reduce God to a superstitious ritual, like a rabbit-foot charm that we rub for good luck. I know of no one who does so purposely or hatefully. Trying to fit God into one of many compartments in our highly organized and "together" lives comes more as a matter of carelessness, a prosperity-induced spiritual coma.

We cannot sharpen the sword of our faith without the friction of conflict and trial. With every struggle people face, every trial, God provides an opportunity for growth, character development, and a deepened spiritual foundation.

Please do not misunderstand me. I find nothing wrong about living a good life with healthy relationships, or with seeking to make the best of every opportunity God sends our way. Neither do I believe that *anyone* lives without some sort of struggle or brokenness. We need not create difficulties to test our faith. We simply need to acknowledge what struggles already exist and look to our Lord to walk in and through them with us.

Quite often our most shameful difficulties can turn out to be cause for the greatest spiritual growth. The converse also holds true. Sometimes there are those from among our most celebrated blessings that can reach out and zap us with unexpected difficulty.

MY STORY

I looked forward to a restful afternoon on that day I traveled to Walmart with my husband, Ben, and several others from our church family with whom we were spending our vacation. Ben took Alethea with him so that I could have some me time strolling around and shopping. I meant to pick up a few summer outfits on my way to some of the other departments. I knew my size, and I had a basic idea of what I wanted, so the whole process of choosing the clothes should not have taken more than about five minutes, tops.

I did not expect the company of two darling ladies from our group, both experienced mothers and grandmothers with more common sense than I cared to share at that moment. Normally I love company when I shop, especially adult female company. However, at that point in my life I preferred to shop alone when picking out clothes. This lessened my shame and embarrassment when my preferred sizes inevitably failed to fit me.

You see, I was what they call a "plus-sized" woman. This is my kind way of saying that since first getting pregnant with my little girl a few years back, my clothing size had steadily increased from a number comparable to my shoe size to one dangerously close to my age. (I was not getting any younger.) As much as I enjoyed the company of my friends, I could muster no enthusiasm for modeling my ever-expanding (and sagging) waistline, another failure with every pound.

I quickly picked out my clothes and started on my way to the electronics department when dear, sweet Anne spoke up.

"Aren't you going to try them on? You could model them for us, and we can help you pick out the best outfit."

Instant fear seized my heart. For the average woman this might seem a reasonable, even fun request. I, on the other hand, cringed at the inevitable onset of humiliation and torture that this ritual would bring me.

I managed to reply to Anne with a calm, "Oh, no, I'm fine. I know my size. I'm sure these will fit."

Really, I was even okay with having tight clothes at home—nothing a good, long shirt couldn't cover. Honestly, I would rather have paid for pants that did not fit than have to display my figure—which seemed to grow larger with every moment—to all who walked by.

"No, Karen, you definitely need to try these on. Clothes are cut differently, and you won't know if this will look good on you until you see it." She had that adamant, motherly look in her eye that said, "I know what I'm talking about. Don't even try to argue."

So much for my leisurely afternoon.

Maybe, just maybe, every outfit would fit well enough that I would only need one trip to the dressing room. Despite my best hopes, this was not the outcome.

In some cases, I needed to go up as many as four sizes from my original choice. Imagine my own personal mortification when even the dressing-room attendant began chiming on the ever-familiar refrain, "No, you'll need a bigger size. Those are definitely too tight on you."

About three years and two hundred dressing-room visits later (at least it seemed that long), I finally broke free from the plus-sized department with two outfits. As we walked to the check-out aisles, Anne and I held a conversation with our eyes.

Her smile said to me "See, that wasn't so bad. You got a few nice outfits out of it. Now wasn't that fun?"

I turned to hide my teary-eyed, exasperated look that responded "Fun? No way. *This was the worst day of my life.*" I asked Ben to pay as I ran to the bathroom to compose myself.

A trip to the doctor the following week confirmed the cause of my dressing-room anguish. Normally I cannot muster the courage to look at the number that appears on the scale. This time I looked intently, determined that this figure would eventually be a cause for rejoicing. The more I weighed at that moment, the greater the victory I could report at losing such a large amount of weight.

Looking at the scale, my wide eyes got even larger. As I noted my new weight, my mind raced back to the days of courtship with my husband. During those months I had lost a significant amount of weight, and I kept in my mind that poundage to which I would never return. The number I saw on that scale at the doctors far surpassed my "never again" weight, exceeding it by well over fifty pounds.

Yikes! My husband and daughter are always quick to remind me that I am a beautiful woman of God, but at that point I felt more like Jabba the Hutt, that freaky alien creature from the Star Wars movies that looked like a talking mountain of lard. I quickly created an attack plan to win the battle of the bulge. I envisioned myself a year later, enjoying the same sort of emotional victory celebration that I saw on those reality weight-loss shows.

How had I let things get this bad? I could easily blame my weight on my metabolic disorder, or the tremendous stress I experienced from a demanding job and a small child, among other things. Or perhaps it was my sporadic eating habits, and the fact that I could count on my hands the number of times I had broken a sweat over the past year.

These habits had to stop. I had to start exercising. I was determined to tip the scales in the opposite direction, no matter what it took.

Easier said than done.

I, of course, hit the ground running, immediately signing up for a membership at the local ladies' gym and embarking on a health food shopping spree. For the first two or three weeks I did an excellent job getting up as early as 5:00 a.m. to hit the gym, hit the sauna, and hit the healthy foods.

Within less than a month reality hit back. Exhaustion set in as I kept an impossible schedule to make up for the two-plus hours it took daily to travel and work out at the gym on the other side of town. (I thought that working out was supposed to give me *more* energy.) Already running on a twelve-to-sixteen-hour time deficit a week from going to the gym, I found it impossible to take the extra time needed to prepare the healthier foods I should have been eating.

Then came the busy time at Ben's work, my own perpetual out-of-town business trips, the school events for our daughter, the daily family mini-crises, and every other possible roadblock to health that I could imagine, not to mention all of the friends and family who were now starting to miss me. This new healthy lifestyle seemed to be hurting me more than it helped. No wonder the United States is the most overweight nation in the world! Given the pressures of daily life in this culture, we don't seem to have a fighting chance.

New plan: Ben and I would quit our jobs, move to South America, and live among some tribal nation that had no access to outside communication, motorized vehicles, or ice cream. Surely, I would be able to get in shape there. If only I had thought of this idea two years previously, before signing those mortgage papers. (I hear that creditors will go even to the ends of the earth to find a person.) So much for my serenity plans.

Given my recent reality check, and with South America safely out of reach, I started praying about the issue. I really wanted some golden key that would just make the problem go away. I would even fantasize that perhaps some doctor would find an enormous benign tumor in my stomach, which when taken out would render me one hundred pounds lighter and in perfect health.

God did not give me a tumor or a quick cure. God did remind me of the truth.

GOD'S STORY

Over and over throughout my struggle with weight, self-image, and general identity issues, God has reminded me of the great personal struggle of the apostle Paul in the Bible's New Testament. Scriptures leave no clue as to the nature of Paul's struggle, other than to characterize it with the title "thorn in the flesh."

Whatever it was, this "thorn in the flesh" of which he spoke, it was enough to transform this proud man into a miserable beggar, pleading repeatedly (like a child, I imagine) for the Lord to take it away. I do not imagine that Paul, this selfless missionary, asked the Lord for much on his own behalf. I also do not suspect that the Lord denied Paul many of the few things he requested for himself. So, this perpetual refusal of relief must have driven him nearly mad.

Here stood the greatest missionary of all time, a spiritual giant by anyone's account. He spoke with fearless boldness in the face of intense persecution, lived through unspeakable horrors with a heart full of joy, and repented with unmatched humility that utterly conquered the sting of his past life of Christian-killing.

Paul literally endured decades of almost continual discrimination and hardship, including blindness, several assassination attempts, beatings, shipwrecks, jail, hunger, betrayal, and the list goes on. Yet he seemed to come out of each one of these things with greater joy and emboldened faith. He did so without pay, all while making his living as a tentmaker on the side. I know of many days wherein a full workday in itself will tire me out; yet his message and tireless efforts reflected an unmistakable supernatural energy, one that no earthly pressure could stifle.

It seemed that nothing could break this man, nothing could get him down. Yet something did. In light of his other triumphs, I cannot imagine what on earth could have done this.

What holy wisdom the Bible displays by declining to name Paul's difficulty. Here the unspoken becomes universal. Were Paul to mention, for example, a physical sickness, some who read might say, "Well that's just his body. This can't apply to my *real* struggle with lust."

On the other hand, should he mention a spiritual battle, or a relationship issue, some might feel tempted to disregard them as "weak issues compared to my battle with cancer." Human nature often leads us to view our problems as the worst in the world, viewing everyone else's grass as greener.

Because the thorn symbolizes a weakness known to no one, it at the same time represents everyone's challenges. It could be a financial problem, a sickness, or a wayward child. It is an addiction, an indefinable spiritual battle, or a propensity for self-hatred. It defines all those things we do not always see in others, but that we fight within ourselves daily. Most blessedly, our thorns are those battles which beat us down to our knees, compelling us to seek our heavenly Daddy for the grace to endure that which we cannot conquer in our own strength.

By the grace of God, I have never struggled with drugs, alcohol, pornography, or the more heavily stigmatized addictions. Nor have I ever really faced any serious health condition or major physical challenges. My blessings extend to a healthy up-bringing, a loving and committed husband and daughter, a good base of solid friends and support, and a phenomenal church fellowship. God has blessed me in many very visible ways.

However, I am sure I know exactly how those people who fight these addictions, ailments, and other personal challenges feel. Obesity is my thorn. To me, battling weight issues feels something like walking up an extremely icy hill, wearing shoes that have no tread. It is all I can do not to lose ground (or *gain*, in this instance), let alone move forward.

When I am most deeply entrenched in this battle, I often find it hard not to feel angry, ugly, inadequate, paralyzed, and hopeless to move forward, among other things. It is not that I do not have other issues, but none other so violently threatens to rip apart and crucify my spirit.

Maybe in the end, that is the point. Maybe I need to let it crucify my spirit, to make room for the full indwelling of God. At the very least, God must receive the glory in all things.

I hope and pray that I will one day leave this battle completely behind, having discovered my ideal lifestyle of both health and fitness without compromising the needs of those around me. Perhaps I will. Maybe God's grace will take this thorn away from me.

However, it is possible that this will be a life-long struggle, no matter what my size or weight. Whatever the case, God's grace will abound amidst and through this thorn, not despite it, and God's grace will *always* be sufficient.

To this day I cannot say that I have fully and consistently achieved my weight and health goals, but this I can say: I am still not a small woman, but I am smaller now than I was in that doctor's office. I am no health fanatic, but I am eating better. I do not keep a perfect schedule, but I rest more and work more reasonable hours. My life has not yet achieved full success, but I am moving forward. I am a work in progress. I am a work of grace.

> *Lord*, use me in and through this battle, and help me to see your perfect, holy face in the midst of my own imperfection. Lord, help me to accept that I am accepted and to see myself in truth, as your beautiful child. When others look at me, may they see not fat or skinny, healthy or sick, rich or poor, but rather a reflection of your holy and perfect love. As I learn to accept your unconditional love, may I also receive life's struggles as an opportunity to walk by faith in you.

YOUR STORY

Read and reflect upon 2 Corinthians 12:1–10. Then consider the following questions:

1. What do you think Paul's thorn was? Was it something familiar to you? How do you think Paul dealt with it?

2. Name your thorn. What (or who) antagonizing force in your life seems unbeatable, insurmountable, and just won't go away, no matter what you do?

3. Dealing with our thorns often demands more attention than we should give, takes our mind off the thing God would have us prioritize. Conversely, they also give us an opportunity to draw near to God in faith and dependence. The difference between the two is entirely up to us. Do you allow your thorns to pull you away from God in distraction or toward God in faith?

4. Think about some of the things that your life struggles have shown, or can show, you about God's grace and protection. Take some time to pray and rejoice in weakness with Paul, thanking God for using this to make the Lord's power perfect in your own life.

CHAPTER 10

How the Shack Became a Palace
Unappreciated Grace - The House, Part II

Give thanks in all circumstances.
1 Thessalonians 5:18

OUR STORY

An old proverb states that familiarity breeds contempt. But the word contempt does not quite cover it for most of us. More accurately, familiarity breeds indigestion.

Our growing relationships somewhat parallel a growing baby in the womb. As it receives nurture it expands, putting pressure on other bodily organs. Eventually, the stomach copes with the space crunch by evicting some of its acid into the esophagus. The result? Heartburn that could kill a cow. And let's be honest. We have all felt that bad taste in our mouths brought about by the people whom we know and love most.

I doubt that this painful bout of acid reflux itself has led many, if any of us as expectant mothers, to dislike or reject the growing life inside of us. We simply grew quite weary with its side effects. Such should be the case with life in general.

I find it perplexing how much more positive of an attitude we generally exhibit toward the people, things, and situations whom we barely know. It's not that we don't appreciate and love our spouses, children, other family, and close friends very deeply. My family always owns my heart. They also push my buttons, buttons about which a stranger could never even know, let alone reach.

Also, I believe that as we grow more at home with those things and people whom we love, or anything for that matter, our familiarity with them seems to dissolve that initial need to always think and act in the most positive manner possible. I suppose that in a very real sense the death of pretense marks the birth of true relationship, whether the object of such be alive or inanimate.

Sometimes I would prefer to keep the pretense.

MY STORY

The idea that familiarity breeds indigestion extends beyond our relationships with other humans. They often include the inanimate resources in our lives that we come to love or despise.

Around the time we first purchased our new home, I described it as a "small but adequate house—a nine-hundred-square-foot, two-bedroom bungalow that could easily accommodate our young family of three." That seemed true enough at the time. The house appeared adequate during the short honeymoon period during and after the purchase.

We knew right away that the house sat in a modest region of town (to say the least), a fact which hardly mattered to us. It had appealed to us more as an investment than a place to call home for any extended period of time.

Not even the crime rates of the surrounding neighborhood alarmed me. We knew that even if we ended up living there, our particular block sat on a rather quiet, dead end street. Also, from the looks of the property inspector's report, the 1950 edifice seemed rather structurally sound to us.

Indigestion quietly crept in with time.

By the next year, our feelings about our purchase had changed quite a bit, as that push of familiarity caused our stomachs to turn. We finally moved in after spending about six months and an additional third of a year's net income recovering from a nightmare tenant, only to find one problem after another with the property. The property inspector had been far less than forthright.

I remember some key moments during that era wherein I did not at all care to hear that ever-familiar question, "How's your new place doing?" I may have politely responded with something like, "There are a few issues, but it's coming along." In my mind I pondered the truth of a more sarcastic response like, "I have discovered the exact location of Purgatory and obtained a mortgage to it."

Truthfully, it did not always work out all that bad. We still had a roof over our heads, with a yard for Ben's gardening and Alethea's play. The low monthly mortgage enabled us to pay off a great deal of debt during a time of oppressive financial struggle for so many others.

At times, however, our little investment struck me as an enormous black hole, sucking all available time, energy, and money. The money we needed (but lacked) to fix all of the issues could have easily purchased us a much better house instead.

To put a positive spin on things, the various challenges we faced provided us with some valuable opportunities for growth. The water damage that defined about half of the house's inner front wall (which did not show up in the initial home inspection report) allowed us to see just how talented and generous Ben's "do-it-yourself" minded father could be with his time and resources.

Ben also got the chance to learn all about roofing when the poor condition of ours compelled him to redo the whole thing. Likewise with plumbing, electrical wiring, and flooring, among other things. (You get the picture.)

I will never forget that period of time wherein the Lord fostered in us an appreciation for running water when a major plumbing problem forced us to live six months without a bathroom sink. Three weeks without a working toilet allowed us ample opportunity to frequently visit with and appreciate our neighbors, and their commodes. The month without a tub or shower provided incentive for us to put our underutilized gym memberships to good use. (We'd take a shower while there.) The entire week and a half without any sort of running water gave us a good reason to stay with family for a few days and catch up. I am not sure how the various gaping large holes in the floor during that time helped us, but I know the Lord used it somehow.

Ben initially received a few unexpectedly unusual opportunities to practice grace with others as he caught several professional street women servicing their clients in our driveway, backyard, and shed. He also got the chance to meet a local celebrity one night when a man walked by and asked if he would like to buy some OxyContin, a narcotic sold mostly at pharmacies. My husband recognized him from the sketch drawing they had been showing on the "Crime Watch" portion of the Channel 12 news for the past few weeks. Coincidently, they had been looking for a man who looked just like him, who had been robbing drug stores all over town for OxyContin.

God once again allowed me to stretch my new forgiveness muscles while picking up the countless beer bottles and cigarette butts deposited in our yard and driveway by those who walked by the fence. They must not have noticed the rather large garbage can next to the ground upon which they threw everything. Perhaps the really loud, vulgar music to which they listened on a nightly basis had an effect on their perception as well. I do not remember ever praying for a patient spirit in the matter, but the Lord surely gave me ample opportunity to earn it. So maybe our street wasn't all that quiet after all.

As our personal spiritual trainer, God really worked out our faith muscles in the area of protection. This began when my father-in-law informed us that our back yard stood less than 150 feet away from the liquor store where he had seen someone murdered over 20 years before. Evidently that liquor store held a record of infamy for crime. In addition to this, those three acres of trees at the dead end, which we thought would help keep the avenue quiet, doubled as a get-away route to many of the numerous criminals who walked the streets just one block over from ours.

We wanted desperately to guard our little girl's sense of safety. We asked in faith for God to close her sleeping ears during the countless violent arguments that occurred in the apartment complex that stood adjacent to our back yard. In order to sleep on those repetitive summer evenings when the quarreling ended in gunfire, we had to believe that God protects those who remain in the Lord's will.

I count the embedded bullets next to our back door as another reminder of God's divine shelter. These came from a shoot-out with police during a drug bust on both of our next-door neighbors (one on each side of us), which providentially happened after we left town to visit Ben's sister for the night. Any other evening, any other time, and we may have stood in the line of fire.

Despite all of this serious indigestion, the Lord continually confirmed in our hearts that our abode provided enough to meet all our earthly needs. It seemed barely enough, but it was enough.

God patiently worked on my heart over these matters. Miraculously, God changed our neighborhood in tandem while changing my own heart. The prostitutes left our yard. Our drug dealer neighbors moved away, or at least a block or two over. The perpetual visitation from local police compelled the gang bangers behind our back yard to take their midnight parties elsewhere, at least for the time being.

In their place we greeted a few elderly saints and another young family. We also discovered some truly excellent people who had lived within a few yards of us all along, people whom we call friends to this day. Slowly, our neighbors began to warmly greet each other by name, to periodically chat over their fences, and to learn things about one another's lives. People would drop what they were doing to give one another a ride to the store or work, or to help out in some way. Our children started to play together. Some of us even went to birthday parties for one another's kids.

Meanwhile, the bottom fell out from the mortgage market, and foreclosure rates spiraled out of control, while simultaneously gas rates spiked. This happened right about at the time that my Ben got a full-time job with good benefits after four-and-a-half years of staying home with our daughter. While most people we knew felt a real financial pinch, for a time we actually enjoyed a better financial situation than we had ever experienced.

We no longer felt the slightest stress of how we would pay our bills, even the unexpected ones. In the times of surprise expense, we tended to have just enough in reserves to pay things off without going into more debt. On the weeks of surplus, which happened most of the time by now, we used the extra to pay down our debt. When I got laid off from my position a year later, the lower cost of housing enabled us to keep our head above water financially despite the huge cut in household income.

I reflected on that beautiful, bigger home that we really wanted, with a price tag of more than twice as much. At the time our credit score dictated that we could have bought it, or even a pricier one. Had we done so, we probably would have lost it, and fallen further in debt with no home to show for it.

At the very least, the struggle to make the high mortgage payments on a "built up" house could have yielded a "broken down" home, and the stress of bills could have worn away at both our personal sense of peace and our marital relationship. By leading us to a smaller, less expensive place, God saved us from all of that.

It finally hit me one day just how truly blessed and happy God had made me in that little shack of a house. The release from heavy financial burdens freed our family to enjoy one another with greater ease and fullness. The familiarity of the neighbors made me happy to come home. In fact, I felt more happiness, peace, and joy in that little abode than I had ever known up until that point. I bowed my head in utmost gratitude for the countless blessings that came into our lives through that purchase.

But it was still a shack. I enjoyed the neighbors, but I carefully avoided the chance to invite over other friends and family. This had something to do with the neighborhood, as I assumed that visiting that particular area of town made many of my friends and family uncomfortable. It had even more to do with my own personal sense of shame at the state of our house.

Frankly, the house just struck me as too ugly, and too small—too all-around inadequate. Several factors, not the least of which was familiarity, turned this once cute small but adequate abode into an embarrassing shack. Though its look needed a good bit of freshening up by now, we decided to hold off on any sort of cosmetic work until we paid off our debt. This only added to the mess of it all.

There were so many unfinished projects: consider the trim-less windows in our living room and bedroom, which exposed their naked 2x4 framing; the stapled-up blanket that hung at the entrance to our preschooler's bedroom, a pathetic excuse for a real door; the cramped and cluttered kitchen/dining room with space for no more than three people at the six-person table; the kitchen and bathroom sink and flooring, or lack thereof. These just name a few of the works in progress that seemed to consume our entire property.

It did not hurt me personally, or even make me uncomfortable to live there. It simply embarrassed me. Though I enjoyed my fence talks with the other neighbors, I felt an inner cringe when even they, who lived in the exact same modeled homes, came into mine. Theirs just always seemed to look so much better than ours.

I am not sure whether I felt more judged or pitied as others walked through our five-room dwelling. I suppose the only real judgment came from my own heart. Still, I tried not to let people inside unless I absolutely had to do so.

Even more than Ben or myself, I did not want other children to judge or make fun of how little our daughter had. She went to preschool with some fairly affluent friends. She always wanted to bring them home or invite them over for sleepovers. I always found ways to change the conversation or put off the plans, fairly confident that their parents would not even allow them in that area of town.

One day while playing with the visiting grandchildren of our next-door neighbor, two cousins, Ali invited them in to see the house. Before I could say no, they had already walked through the kitchen, bathroom, living room, and office and made their way to Ali's bedroom.

Unlike me, little Ali walked through our home with boldness, proudly pointing out all of its finest aspects. She felt most proud to show them around her room, a small compilation of mostly old or cheap toys, books, and dress-up items. Ali joyfully and excitedly showed them around it as if they walked through a fine palace. Oh, for the naiveté of childhood!

The other children struck me as the blatantly honest types, so I braced myself for damage control with my poor, tenderhearted little girl. I imagined her running to me after hearing the truth from her new friends, that the whole house should be knocked down, and her cheap little room, courtesy of the Dollar Tree and the local discount stores, may not have been worth one good toy of theirs.

As I heard both children gasp at Alethea's bedroom, my heart predicted the words that would inevitably come out of their mouths:

"Your sheets don't match your pillowcase."

"You only have three real Barbie Dolls?"

"Did you get all of your toys from the dollar store?"

"You put your toys in a big plastic container? Where's your toy box?"

"Your dress-up clothes have tears in them. You need to throw them out and get new ones."

"Where is your door? What kind of a weirdo has a blanket for a bedroom door?"

You can imagine my surprise when I heard the following conversation instead:

"All of this is yours?" The little girl said with a wide-eyed look of wonderment (or so I imagined).

"Well, yes. It's *my* room," replied my beaming little one.

"Wooooooow!" I heard from both of them.

The little girl's cousin, who stood with them, came out of the room, and with an enthusiastic smile he said to me, "Mam, you have a really nice house." Had I not sensed his sincerity and seen the look in his eye, I would have likely thought he said so in jest.

A few minutes later Ali invited the two to stay for lunch. I again felt embarrassed at our lack of provision, as she gave the invitation only a day or two before our bi-weekly trip to the supermarket. I managed to round up about the last of the "quick food" that I had: some milk, peanut butter and jelly sandwiches, three cheese sticks, and some peanut butter crackers. I also made some instant oatmeal at Ali's request. I just knew this wouldn't do for them, whose grandmother was undoubtedly a much better provider for them.

Still, the children showed great politeness and gratitude. They thanked me excessively, and they even ate the food. The little boy looked at me and said "Ma'am, you are so nice." Then, as I left the kitchen, I heard him whisper something curious to his cousin. "She has so much food in her refrigerator."

I later learned that both of them lived with their siblings' family in a government housing project on the other side of town. The little girl's mother lived there with the boy and his family as they waited and hoped for funding to find an apartment of their own.

At that moment I felt such a strong conviction shoot through my heart that it almost drove me to tears. I thought about the children across the world who count it as great fortune to have even one or two toys, for whom "provision" may mean a few bowls of rice and perhaps a mat upon which to sleep at night.

I thought of the mothers who weep at night for their young daughters, who have been stolen into a sex-trafficking ring. Others cry for their sons, whom guerilla armies have kidnapped and brainwashed for their own militant purposes.

It occurred to me that some people feel blessed when they can even go to the market in safety, without fear of their food being stolen on the way home. Some live in fear of ever speaking their mind. Young women struggle and pray to maintain their virginity, to keep from being raped by insurgents or enemy armies. Some young men fear torture or death because of the color of their skin, the denomination of their belief, or simply for unknowingly standing in the line of fire.

In this very country children in Appalachia suffer severe malnutrition and poverty on a daily basis. Young men in big cities all over the nation join gangs for protection and respect, only to gain the opposite through imprisonment, punishment, and often death. Young women sell or give their bodies away on hopes of feeling valued and loved, only to gain the opposite through abuse and disregard. Consequently, countless children grow up without ever knowing a father's love and protection, and sometimes without even a mother.

At that moment I realized that in every conceivable way our family stood among the richest percentage of humanity in the entire world, and of all time. Yet I had stayed so focused on what we did not have that I forfeited the ability to truly enjoy it. God had given me everything, and yet I allowed Satan to take the joy right from my hands.

That was the day when our shack became a palace.

That day changed me. I did not stop dreaming of better things, and yet these dreams would no longer stifle my present joy. I determined to move forward in gratitude, with an attitude of remembrance. It started me wondering how very many other gifts of God I might forfeit simply by choosing not to recognize them.

GOD'S STORY

From the time of Pentecost, the early church enjoyed a great honeymoon period of prosperity and togetherness. Most churches nowadays would be happy to add a few members a month, or even a few per year. It is all most churches in this country can do to just maintain their congregational numbers without losing members. Imagine *adding* over three thousand willing and on-fire members to a congregation during its first public meeting, as the early church did.

This followed with an increase in both number and spirit on a daily basis, giving the twelve apostles a wonderful new problem. With so many members, representing so much need, they required help in organizing and leading their new flock. In response to the blessed problem, they appointed and anointed the first seven church deacons. Deacon roughly translates to mean servant, so these men acted in the capacity of the church's chief servants, a title of honor and great importance.

Steven stood out among the seven they chose as a man "full of grace and power," who "performed great wonders and signs among the people" (Acts 6:8). A rare combination of wisdom, boldness, humility, and fantastic rhetoric rendered him among the greatest, most powerful members of the early church.

Those who opposed The Way, as they often called the early church, tried to prove Stephen's words wrong, but no one could manage to win a debate against him. Every time someone opposed him, their efforts to discredit him would backfire. Stephen's logic, eloquence, and passion would win more people over to the way of Christ.

Stephen's impact caused great alarm and disturbance among the established members of the synagogue. His enemies eventually brought him before the Sanhedrin, the Jewish ruling council, using false witnesses and trumped-up charges.

Stephen once again spoke boldly and convincingly against his accusers. Using Old Testament history, he effectively exposed them all as the real perpetrators and blasphemers.

Then came the reversal. As the accused became the rightful accuser, the courtroom of legal authorities turned into the outlaws. They furiously rushed at Stephen and killed him barbarically by stoning, winning him the title of the first Christian martyr. "On that day, a great persecution broke out against the church at Jerusalem, and all except the apostles were scattered throughout Judea and Samaria. Godly men buried Stephen and mourned deeply for him. But Saul began to destroy the church. Going from house to house, he dragged off both men and women and put them in prison" (Acts 8:1–3).

Thus ended the honeymoon and began the indigestion.

I wonder how many of the early believers chose to do nothing, to stop believing because of this persecution. Some must have deserted, but from the tone of Acts, it seems that most preferred to leave town rather than leaving their newfound love of Christ.

Comfort was never the rule of the day for most early Christians. For a very long time, increased familiarity with Jesus Christ led to earthly hardship and difficulty, even death. People were displaced from their homes, imprisoned taunted, inaccurately represented. This situation is not unlike many environments for countless Christians around the world even today.

Indigestion.

And yet they were so, so very blessed.

As a result of the persecution in Jerusalem, two major things happened. First of all, the church grew even more: "Those who had been scattered preached the word wherever they went. Philip went down to a city in Samaria and proclaimed the Messiah there. When the crowds heard Philip and saw the signs he performed, they all paid close attention to what he said. for with shrieks, impure spirits came out of many, and many who were paralyzed or lame were healed. So there was great joy in that city" (Acts 8:4–8).

Second, this indirectly set the stage for one of the most miraculous and dramatic conversions of all history. You see, as the church spread abroad, so did the Jewish leader Saul's ambition to annihilate its members.

In a northern trip to Damascus to persecute the Christians there, Saul met the Lord. He received his new name Paul and became the most notable Christian missionary of all time. The impact and conviction from the role he played in Stephen's death caused him to live and preach all the more passionately in his travels.

When faced with heartburn, literally or in relationships, we can do one of three things. We can ignore it. We can also focus on the negativity of it and complain. Both responses usually cause the problem to fester and grow, which will only make the situation worse.

On the other hand, we can decide to look for the blessing in it. Along with this, we can choose to move toward a solution, to eat and live in healthier ways, to work it out. This will ultimately serve to improve both our heartburn and our overall health.

I often tend to take the things and people dearest to me for granted, forgetting just how many blessings God has brought me through them. I all too often complain about life's inconvenience rather than thanking God for life's endless grace. I pray for myself, and for all of us, that we would move toward the strength of mind and heart to see the supernatural blessings of God in our daily hiccups, to see the crisis points on earth as an opportunity to love and grow as citizens within our true home, the Kingdom of Heaven.

Lord, how easily I forget your blessings. Forgive me for taking you for granted. Forgive me for complaining about your many blessings as if they were curses. Lord, please crucify that critical spirit within me, and replace it with the heart of praise toward you, which you so wholly deserve.

YOUR STORY

Read and reflect upon Acts 2:42–47 and 6:1–8:8. Then consider the following questions:

1. What reasons did the early church have to rejoice?

2. What reasons did the early church have to fear and/or despair? What kinds of things happened that might understandably strike fear in their hearts?

3. How did the Lord turn the persecution into a further cause for rejoicing?

4. Think of some part of your life about which you complain. How might the Lord be blessing you in this very area?

5. Now think about your situation in relation to that of those around the world who suffer daily. In comparison with other's difficulties, how important is your cause for complaint?

6. Make a list of the difficulties you have. Then make a list of the countless blessings God has placed in your life. Can you see any reason to praise the Lord right this second? If so, don't hesitate to praise God now.

CHAPTER 11

THE BLESSED BREAKDOWN
Providential Grace

And we know that in all things God works for the good of those who
love him, who have been called according to his purpose.
Romans 8:28

OUR STORY

Have you ever had one of those days when it seems that just about
everything that can go wrong does? Imagine the following scenario:

The alarm clock fails to ring, causing you to wake up almost an
hour late. The kids will not listen to you. You find the stain on the
carpet, courtesy of your "house broken" dog. To top it all off, in your
hurry to get things together, you spill coffee and stain your favorite
shirt. And that's just before you walk out the front door.

Other daily hassles may include the nasty weather, which causes
a major accident, which causes a traffic jam. This makes you even later
for work and that important staff meeting. Since you are late for the
meeting, your boss gives you the worst assignment, the one no one
else who made the meeting on time would take.

This gets you behind in your other work on a major project; only
you cannot work late, because you have promised to meet your in-laws
for dinner. Instead, you decide to work through lunch. This causes
you to accidentally miss that long-anticipated lunch date with an old

friend whom you never see due to your hectic schedules, but to whom you really needed to talk and vent about everything that seems to be going wrong lately.

Right about the time you realize you missed your lunch date, you sneeze. A quick hand to the forehead informs you that the nasty weather effected more than the traffic. You have a high fever. Giving up on any hope for doing anything productive that day, you go home, put on your most comfortable pajamas and crawl under the covers, wondering why you ever even bothered getting out of bed this morning.

We have all been there. Some days just seem like life has broken down on you. Nothing you plan happens, and it seems that everything you plan against does happen. What a waste.

Then again, our perspective may change drastically if we have the courage and patience to look at these happenings through the perspective of divine provision. God tends to see things differently than we do. How blessed are the days when God lends us the eyes of Heaven, enabling us to see our perpetual breakdowns as opportunities to experience God's glory and grace.

MY STORY

Life seems to throw these sorts of monkey wrenches in my own best made plans at the most inopportune times. My car once broke down en route to a speaking engagement. It literally just stopped working as I was driving in the far-left lane of a state highway, well over an hour from home.

Needless to say, the breakdown caused great inconvenience to several people. First of all, the leaders of that church where I had been scheduled to speak had to try and pull together a last-minute plan for the program that I would inevitably fail to make. This came after months of negotiations with the church leaders to determine just the right date for me to present. Evidently, the Lord had another date in mind.

Then there was my husband who, on the tails of his own big event, had to steal away in the middle of the workday, grab our daughter from school, and come to my rescue, having to postpone his own plans to meet with other friends that evening.

Our bank account took a hit as well. Not only did we have to absorb the cost for gas for an extra vehicle to go to and from the location; we also had the fee for repair, the extra cost of eating dinner out that evening, and the lost wages from Ben missing half a day of work.

All of this came just three weeks after we had paid a pretty penny to our own mechanic to make sure my car was in the best possible condition to travel. I learned that a car's alternator could just decide to shut down on a person, giving a mechanic little to no sign of its poor condition even days ahead of time.

Personally, I felt somewhat humiliated about having to ask so many people for help, and for having to cancel the speaking engagement at such short notice. Professionally speaking, the day was a total waste. By all human accounts, I had every right to feel pretty crummy about it all.

Ironically, it was one of the best days I had in a long time.

The key was not so much in what happened, but in how the Lord used it to bring about an awareness of God's grace. In the midst of what could have been a really awful time, God spoke so clearly to me about the Lord's divine provision that I could not help but smile. The perfection of timing, location, and people involved made it impossible for me to consider the design as mere chance.

The car completely shut down less than two hundred yards from a mini-mall. This was the first sign of development for over thirty miles. Had I broken down even a mile or two sooner, I would have been left stranded on the side of the road, dangerously inhibiting the flow traffic in an area where there was not so much as a shoulder on which to park.

I also shut down precisely during a brief lull in otherwise steady traffic. This enabled me to safely coast over two lanes of traffic, into the parking lot, and into a parking space without getting hit. Had this happened even seconds later I would have been stuck in the far-left lane at the first traffic light for miles, without the power to turn on my hazard lights. At best I could have caused a traffic jam. At worst it could have caused an accident and been badly injured.

Then there were the people God sent me. Ben's boss let him leave work immediately and allowed him to take a company car to come out and get me, knowing that I was driving our family's only personal vehicle at the time. One of the employees I knew at a local church arranged for me to get help from a service station that worked on that church's vehicles.

Even strangers helped. It came as no small miracle that the service station the local church used was located less than a quarter of a mile from my broken-down car. One of the mechanics from the shop offered to come out to my car on his own time, at no charge, to check it out.

Then came the miracle of the resurrected alternator. My car started up and ran literally just long enough to get me to the entrance of the mechanic's shop, at which point I again coasted, conveniently downhill, to the mouth of the garage. I can only imagine the extra time and expense it would have wasted had I needed to call a tow truck to carry me 250 yards.

The mechanic mentioned that he would not be able to install the alternator until the next day, so I knew we would need to plan on making another three-hour round trip the following evening to pick it up. Thankfully and unexpectedly, the service center's office manager promptly tracked down the right part and rearranged the mechanic's schedule to allow for him to finish work on my car that day.

The mechanic fixed my car within two hours. He finished it just ten minutes before their closing time, and five minutes before my husband arrived. What's more, the fact that we had just deposited an outside check into our account the day before enabled us to pay for the repairs in full without having to go further into debt.

As the greatest gift and miracle God gave me that day, the breakdown provided me with extra time to enjoy my husband and daughter. All three of us felt the strain that came from a hectic couple of weeks of work, church activity, and helping out friends. However, we could not drop any of our projects for the next week or two to create space for each other. This blessed breakdown gave us the needed room in our schedule to spend time together as a family.

We agreed that even though I could drive the car home, it was good for Ben to take the drive out. He wanted to follow me home, in case anything else happened with the car. This enabled me to spend a solid hour talking to my daughter Ali on the way home, and it created time for us to stop for dinner together and walk around a bit. Had I not broken down, I would not have gotten back home that night until about midnight, long after Alethea and Ben fell asleep.

My Lord personally crafted this blessed breakdown to remind me afresh of God's ability to bless in and through all circumstances.

GOD'S STORY

When God's Apostle Paul wrote to the church of Rome, he spoke of much greater problems than mere car trouble. The church in Rome faced large scale systemic oppression and injustice.

By the time of Paul's letter, the Roman Jews and the new Jewish sect coming to be known as Christians had already suffered mass expulsion from the city of Rome twice within a fifty-year period, having just recently come back from their second deportation. The city of Rome was known in the day for its multi-ethnic, tolerant atmosphere long before the "metropolitan feel" came into mainstream popularity. Yet Roman rule provided little room for freedom with the small, misunderstood group who worshipped an executed man whom they claimed had risen from the dead.

Paul's commentary on present suffering seemed almost prophetic. For within only a few years after his letter, the Christians all over the Roman Empire suffered a mass martyrdom, perhaps an attempt at genocide, at the hands of Emperor Nero. Nero sought a scapegoat when others accused him of burning down Rome. At the hands of such unfair accusations as cannibalism, the early Christians of all ages (even kids) in Rome bore the most horrendous and demeaning deaths, including being ripped apart by lions for the entertainment of a cheering crowd.

Paul also spoke autobiographically of this suffering, for though he had not yet been to Rome to personally share the gospel, he would soon visit to partake of his own form of persecution through unjust trials, and years of house arrest without a single indictment of wrongdoing. He had already endured numerous stonings, betrayals, false arrests, and a shipwreck, among other things, throughout the Roman world.

What an incredible amount of faith it must have taken Paul to recognize God's work in all things—for even *Paul's* good—despite his continual persecution and suffering. It would take someone with Paul's background and credibility to effectively deliver such a message of encouragement to the church of Rome.

Truthfully, Paul's persecution and suffering continued until the point of his death. And the Christians to whom Paul wrote faced persecution and suffering that would only get worse in a few years' time, and that would not stop for many of them until the point of their own deaths. As dire as this sound, they could still take hope in knowledge of the fact that ultimately all of the suffering would lead to their good. To use Paul's words: "Therefore we do not lose heart. Though outwardly we are wasting away, yet inwardly we are being renewed day by day. For our light and momentary troubles are achieving for us an eternal glory that far outweighs them all. So we fix our eyes not on what is seen, but on what is unseen, since what is seen is temporary, but what is unseen is eternal" (2 Corinthians 4:16–18).

Even today Christians all over the world suffer greatly in their bodies for their beliefs, and yet they take honor and joy in their service for Christ. Oh, for that faith! And yet I admit I would not want to go through all the trials that it would take to bring me to that point.

While we may not be able to imagine the pain of the early (and current) Christian martyrs, I think we may be equally unaware of the extent of their hope and joy, which far exceed human pleasure or understanding. Those blessings extended beyond their own lives.

Amid Paul's persecution his ministry thrived, and his joy only seemed to increase. God worked this for Paul's good. Amid the early persecution in Rome, the church thrived and grew exponentially. Others must have seen some incredible benefits to this life to want to join it despite the oppression. The church often continues to thrive and grow most in areas of persecution.

God worked even the horrible persecution to their good, both then and in the long run. Rome continues as one of the spiritual strongholds in the church, and Paul is still seen as arguably the most effective Christian missionary of all time.

You see, as the expert artist, the Lord can use all shades of life, no matter how blinding or dismal, to make a masterpiece out of us. The size of the problem makes no difference. Famines, epidemics, and holocausts present no contest compared to God's plan. At the opposite extreme, no matter how small the problem—from a broken-down car to a broken nail or even an unkind word—God will use it for the greater good of those who love the Lord.

This begs a difficult question in my own life. If Paul could praise the Lord working all things together even amidst the most difficult kind of human life, why can't I praise God through all of my own petty problems?

When my car broke down, I had the unusual presence of mind to say "God, please show me your glory in this." That made all of the difference. Why is that not my reaction in all things? I am not sure if I can answer this fully, but this I know: I believe that God does use everything for the benefit for those who love the Lord, and the more I choose to claim this, remember this, and praise God for it, the happier I will be.

Lord, I praise you for the blessed breakdowns you bring about in my life. Thank you for life's unique little interruptions that you allow in order to meet my needs in the midst of the earthly chaos that I create for myself. You truly are love. You truly are sovereign. You truly are God. May my heart learn to rejoice no matter what, knowing that it is all for Your glory, and You will use it for my good.

YOUR STORY

Read and reflect upon Romans 8:18–39. Then consider the following questions:

1. What are some ways that God worked things together for the good of the church in Rome? How did God work things together for Paul's good?

2. Romans 8:28 says that God works all things together "for the good of those who love him." Do you truly love God? If not, what is keeping you from doing so?

3. Think of something over the past few days that you found mildly annoying, like being cut off on the road, or dropping something on your toe. How do you think God might use that for God's glory and your good?

4. Think of the biggest problem you have faced (or are facing) over your lifetime? Can you see how God has worked that for your good? If not, can you think of how the Lord might eventually work that for your good?

5. Can you think of any other circumstances where God worked out a seemingly bad situation for your good? Spend some time sharing about this.

CHAPTER 12

HOWIE
Consuming Grace

*Love the Lord your God with all your heart and with all your soul and
with all your strength.*
Deuteronomy 6:5

OUR STORY

I think I know what makes fairytales so popular. It has to do with
one common thread that runs through almost all of them. I do not
mean the happily ever after ending, though a positive conclusion to
a story always does my heart good. Nor do I refer to the emphasis on
inner virtue and valor. Though admirable, you can find that within
most literature.

Think about these fairytale titles for a minute: "The Prince and
the *Pauper*," "Beauty and the *Beast*," "Snow White and the Seven
Dwarfs," "The *Hunchback* of Notre Dame." In virtually every fairy tale
you read, you will find a person of uncommonly great virtue and value
who comes from the most unlikely place.

The stories' greatest heroes and heroines come to us as commoners at best, outcasts at worst. Then through the plot of the story, their
inner beauty somehow rises to the surface, until people everywhere
finally see them for the proverbial heroes and royalty that they have
always been.

We love to visualize these stories as if they defined our own lives. A big part of us longs to live the fairytale, so we learn to thrive vicariously through the story's characters. Some of us want the handsome prince to come rescue us. Some of us want to be that handsome prince. We secretly desire for others to see our hidden beauty and value.

Ironically, we often find it difficult to see the hidden beauty in others. We see the beast of a boss at work, the hunchback secretary who won't leave us alone, that pesky little dwarf of a repair man who will not stop cussing, the bothersome, drunken pauper on the street who always asks us for money. Our hearts find it much easier to assign value to the hypothetical characters in literature than to the people who annoy and inconvenience us in our everyday lives.

Oh, for the eyes to see them as God sees them! To the Lord, each one of these is a sleeping beauty, needing only to awaken to God's acceptance of them, and the Lord's plan for their lives.

Every once in a while, though rarely, someone identifies that diamond in the rough, that unsung hero. As in fairytales, they usually come from the least expected places. Getting to know how powerfully God can use these generally disregarded individuals to bring about God's will on earth is enough to change the way we look at everything.

MY STORY

From the beginning, Howie always struck me as the friendly sort. So it came as no surprise to me when he chose to sit next to me during the church service that Sunday morning. With him beside me, I knew that this morning's service would be anything but boring.

This was my fourth or fifth visit to that small congregation, where I had been scheduled to do some ongoing training with the members. Getting out to meet and build relationships with people in the local churches was unquestionably my favorite part of the job. I particularly loved participating in gatherings such as these, who would welcome me as one of their own.

There was something different about Howie, a reality that screamed at me on this particular morning. He inched closer and closer to me, to the point of literally squashing me into the corner of the pew. Then he put his arm around me, grabbed my keys, and proceeded to smile a sort of a dreamy-eyed smile while staring directly at me throughout most of the worship service. The warm welcome began to heat up a bit beyond my own comfort zone.

It seems important here to note that Howie was a person of extremes. As a mentally challenged man in his early thirties, he lacked the skill to do many things well, if at all. He spoke only a few words, with little to no sign-language ability to augment his communication. He could not read, write, or even sing a simple melody to a recognizable tune. He required heavy assistance to carry out some of the daily functions that most of us would count as natural, if not easy.

But what Howie did, he did extremely well.

For one thing, he was a wonderful thief. He would craftily approach to hold your hand like a friend. Then while reaching for a hug he would finagle you out of your car keys, purse, or whatever else you happened to have on your person. Before you knew what hit you, he would be down the hall or out the door with that unforgettable smile on his face. He once got ambitious and tried to steal my arm right off my body. Fortunately, his was a burglary of jest. He always eventually returned the booty to its proper owner.

He could also belch like nobody's business. Within just a few short visits, I noted his gift for belting them out right at the most inopportune times in the service—generally during prayer time, an altar call, or one of the more dramatic points of the sermon. These were no small noises. I am fairly certain that some earthquakes have begun from less agitation.

Along with the belching came the loud yelling, again with impeccable timing. There were the general squeals of joy that came as he saw someone whom he knew, or even a stranger, come to think of it. He seemed to just like seeing people. He loved to use one of his few words, no, at the top of his lungs as a response for the entire room when the pastor asked such things as, "Are there any questions?" or, "Is there anyone who would like to receive Jesus today?"

Then there was the smile, that trademark smile. I do not believe I ever saw him without it. More importantly, the smile seemed to reach deep beyond his eyes, back to the very depths of his soul. It rendered his joy both endearing and infectious. The exception to this for me was when the smile came in the form of a starry-eyed stare, less than six inches from my face throughout the bulk of a Sunday morning worship service.

Most importantly, Howie knew how to moan. He moaned deep and full. The more excited he got, the louder he wailed. These noises did not reflect any sort of pain or anxiety. Howie moaned as a joyful noise to the Lord. To the untrained ear, this "joyful noise" of his might come across as a highly awkward annoyance and distraction from worship. On the contrary, I am certain that in Heaven's eyes it falls among the most beautiful human sounds God has ever heard.

As I sat in that service—squashed in the corner of the pew, trying not to make eye contact, and wondering how I might get my keys back and breath—we began to sing these timeless words penned by Edward H. Joy:

> *Jesus, Thou art everything to me*
> *Jesus, Thou art everything to me*
> *All my lasting joys are found in Thee*
> *Jesus, Thou art everything to me*[4]

When I first heard Howie's holy moan, I did not recognize it for what it was. For a moment I wondered what caused him such pain. Then, as I noticed his raised hand and smiling face, God allowed me to see and hear the sound beyond my human senses.

Right there it occurred to me as clear as day that without being able to write, read, say, or even hum that chorus correctly Howie meant every word of it with every fiber of his being, probably more than any one of us in that room ever would. Jesus truly meant the world to Howie, whose only joy was found in God.

---

4 Edward H. Joy was a Salvation Army Officer from the late 1800s and early 1900s. The words to the verses of this hymn (he only wrote the verse, not the chorus, and not the music) are in *The Salvation Army Songbook*.

At that one holy moment, I struggled to keep back my own tears of conviction and shame. For all of his limitations, I knew that Howie kept God's law, both in letter and spirit, better than I. For all his distracting characteristics, I knew that he worshipped God with complete joy and self-abandonment. And for all of his staring, his look of love carried a nearly unmatchable integrity of heart. I knew then that for me to look at Howie's face that moment meant to look into the very nature of Christ.

Howie did eventually give me back my keys. Along with restoring the access to my car, his example unlocked a new understanding and conviction that allowed me to travel more deeply into the heart of God.

GOD'S STORY

Through Moses's instructions to the Israelites God has provided us all with a simple yet effective formula for the greatest sort of heroes of the faith.

The younger generations of Israelites had been homeless, penniless, and directionless for their entire lives. They had known no scene other than the ground under their feet, eaten nothing but manna and quail, and thus far heard nothing but an unfulfilled promise from their leader Moses that it would not always be this way.

Then one day they saw something new at the end of the horizon. The rich and prosperous land that the Lord God had promised to their ancestors came within sight, and suddenly within reach. It's hard to imagine how wonderful and truly awe-inspiring the sight of a skyline, walls, trees, and grass might look to a people for whom endless wilderness had been the only permanent fixture ever.

As the young Israelites gathered to hear Moses's address before crossing into the Promised Land, they must have expected to hear some new words of wisdom. On the contrary, the content of Moses's final address before his own death, and the beginning of their new lives, all revolved around just one word of advice—remember.

Specifically, Moses warned them against forgetting the Lord as their only source of strength. His address totaled more than just a mere summation of rules and regulations. In a very real sense, he gave only one rule, to remember love. Every other stroke of God's law served to show them how to do so within their context.

Moses drove this point home by speaking the most important and unifying command of all Scripture. Jewish culture refers to the words of Deuteronomy 6:4–5 as the "Shema," a title derived from the Hebrew form of the first word of the passage. Roughly translated it means "hear," "listen up," or "pay close attention." "Hear O Israel: the LORD our God, the LORD is one. Love the LORD your God with all your heart and with all your soul and with all your strength" (Deuteronomy 6:4–5).

Moses basically said "Guys, pay close attention to what I am about to say: God, the same God who has been with us all along, is the only true God, the only thing you will ever need, and thus the only one whom you should ever worship. Whatever you do, never forget to love God with everything you've got" (author's paraphrase).

The language Moses used for *how* they should do so merits some attention. He said that they should love the Lord:

*With all their **heart***—In this verse's original Hebrew language and culture, the heart *(levav)* symbolized the very core of existence and life, a sort of a combination between how we might see the heart, mind, and soul together nowadays.

*With all their **soul***—The Hebrew word *nephesh*, which we translate to mean soul, would make no distinction between the body and the spirit. To love God with our whole *nephesh* means to love God with absolutely everything we are, physical, intellectually, emotionally, and spiritually, from the inside out.

*With all their **strength***—The word *modah*, which Deuteronomy 6:5 translates to mean strength, may also mean stature, capacity, authority, or resources. This actually extends beyond us to every outside resource over which we may exert any influence.

In essence, to love the Lord with all our heart, soul, and strength means to love God from the very core of our being, throughout every iota of our lives, and even beyond ourselves, reaching out to the world around us.

So important was and is this concept that fifteen hundred years later, when the religious leaders asked Jesus about the greatest commandment, he mentioned these very verses, noting that this forms the basis for everything God requires of us (Matthew 22:37). Modern Christians often refer to this as "The Great Commandment," the single greatest direction of all Scripture.

So important was this concept to the Israelites that they taught their people to memorize it word for word. They would sing it in songs. They would bind the words to their foreheads. They would write it on their doorposts. They would even teach their children that they were to utter these sentences as their very last words, using their very last breath of life.

Yet they still forgot. Somehow in their working out this law of love which Moses had shared, they became attached to the law and forgot the love. Without the love, the law lost its power, and eventually people began to pick and choose which ordinances they wanted to follow.

They also ignored God's prophets, who warned them repeatedly to repent. After God got their attention by allowing them to fall prey to their own mistakes, they would cry out for help and briefly change their ways, only to soon fall back into their own sinfulness and pride, once again forgetting their first love.

This same cycle of sin defines the story journey throughout the Bible. It is the story of humanity. This is why we need Jesus so badly. If left to our own devices, we would continually be like dogs returning to our own vomit. (A gross, but biblical illustration. See Proverbs 26:11.) It is sick. It is stomach turning. And but for the grace of God through Jesus Christ, it would be our destiny.

Those of us who accept God's gift of grace through Jesus have available the freedom to love God with our everything—abandoning all other fears and concerns, and knowing that our Lord will take care of us. I must admit that though I know this promise, I do not always personally claim it.

In fact, as I write this, I allow a number of needless concerns to keep me from a good night's sleep. I must again allow God to crucify these worries within me, just as Christ's death crucified the power of sin, so that I may more fully focus on God alone.

I have often looked to many spiritual mentors for guidance about my own personal walk with Christ. I try to emulate the learned and eloquent leaders who carry themselves with the most profound dignity and speak with high-impacting, well-spoken truths.

For a moment during that church service, and at my best moments, I believe, my priorities changed. I think that if I really do want to learn how to be like Jesus, I must begin by following Howie's example.

Every once in a while, I meet a person who seems to truly live out the call of the *Shema*, that completely unadulterated love and commitment that abandons everything but the Lord alone. That is what makes my friend Howie so very special.

Howie is my hero.

Lord, it amazes me how you use the seemingly weak things of this world to shame the strong. I long to love you with the purity and faith of those less fortunate than me. Yet my heart holds me back. This is not your will, Lord. Please continue to purge me and teach my heart, so that I may love you as I should, as you deserve.

YOUR STORY

Read and reflect upon Deuteronomy 6:1–10. Then consider the following questions:

1. How do you think the Israelites might have felt as they heard Moses's words in this final address before entering into the Promised Land?

2. Given all the miracles and help they had directly experienced from the Lord, why do you think it is that the Israelites kept forgetting and falling away from God?

3. What do you think it is within each of us that causes us to keep forgetting and falling away from the Lord?

4. Do you have any Howies in your life? When they come around, do you generally view them as a nuisance or a blessing? Do you generally *treat* them as a nuisance or a blessing?

5. How do you think your life would be different if you truly loved the Lord all the time with your everything, inside and outside? What would it take to get you to that point?

CHAPTER 13

My Daddy, My Fortress
Protecting Grace

The Lord Almighty is with us; the God of Jacob is our fortress.
Psalm 46:7

OUR STORY

Tsunamis in the South Pacific, suicide bombings in the Middle East, terrorist bombings on domestic soil, Midwest Tornadoes, 9/11, California wildfires, AIDS, sex trafficking, numerous school shootings, civil unrest and war, COVID-19, and the list goes on and on.

Both natural and man-made disasters seem to have plagued our nation and world over the past few decades. Some have taken this as a sign pointing to the end of time. Others see it as a fitting and rightful punishment from God in response to the general waywardness and evil within the human race. Ecologists may count this as the logical consequences of hundreds of years of disregard for our environment and ourselves. Some ignore it all, assured that this merely comes as a random coincidence of happenings within the ongoing cycle of life.

Most of us do not know quite what to make of it all. Two things remain certain: we cannot change the fact that any of this happened, and not a single one of us has the power to undo the damage that has been done—at least not on our own. In a sense, this great tapestry of tragedy painted on the horizon of humanity seems to point out one universal truth: humanity is relatively powerless.

This does not mean that we cannot do anything. To say that we suffer complete powerlessness would remove from personal ownership the consequences of our deeds, both good and bad. Many of the above-mentioned tragedies and the deaths to which they led came about, at least in part, by some human neglect or mismanagement. On the other hand, God brings about some beautiful results through the faithful and loving actions of people. The key is to remember that God, not people, brings the results.

Unfortunately, more often than not, our menial actions serve to feed our illusion of control. We easily forget that if God wants to do something, or to allow something to happen, there is usually nothing we can do to stop it. If God determines that something will never happen, then none of our best-laid plans and efforts can lead events in the opposite direction. And if for some reason beyond our understanding God allows Satan the power to bring some sort of storm in our life, only God can stop the wind. Sometimes the best we can do is weather the storm, then pick up the pieces. Though we can appeal for change and hope that God agrees with us, we simply cannot overpower the source of all power.

At first glance these realities seem somewhat morbid, even hopeless. On the contrary, they give cause for a greater hope. In knowing that we do not hold the power, we can release ourselves from the pressure to save the world, to make all things better. God has never expected this of us. Why expect something of ourselves that we cannot give? If we could save the world, or even ourselves, God would not have sent Jesus to do it for us.

In reality, those who serve Christ do have great power and authority in this life. But that power and authority are completely subordinate to God's sovereignty. Sometimes God will empower us to move mountains, bring healing, and work miracles. Sometimes it's all we can do to desperately cling to our faith while the world around us comes crashing down, and all of our best efforts seem to fall short of addressing the physical pain and suffering of it all.

God's Word calls us forth as "more than conquerors through him who loved us" (Romans 8:37), and promises astounding victories and healings within this lifetime. However, it serves us well to remember that our greatest call is not to dominance, but to love. Our primary goals are not to accomplish things and prevent bad things from happening, but rather to love God and to allow God's love to flow in and through us to others. The true victory does not come through lack of struggle and suffering, but rather amidst it.

The reality of suffering and weakness need not diminish our authority or hope, because both extend beyond this life. True authority and hope both rely on a God who is eternally in control even when we in our limited perspective cannot see it right now. We can take the greatest eternal hope in the fact that the infinite, all-loving, all-powerful Creator of the universe holds all life in balance, working out every single, minuscule detail for the good of those who love God, and to God's glory (Romans 8:28).

I do not offer these thoughts as an excuse to keep from doing what God calls us to do. Rather, let us remain encouraged that our calling is much easier than many of us make it out to be. The Lord does not call us to *do for* God, but rather to *be with* God, to rest in our heavenly provider's embrace, and to allow God to do through us. Everything that we do, say, and feel can come as an overflow of the empowerment of God's embrace and the knowledge that God has things under control.

What a great way to live! If only we could remember to keep it that simple.

MY STORY

The Lord has repeatedly used my earthly parents to remind me of my heavenly Father's provision. Several years ago, my parents visited us during our brief residence on the coast. Since living near the ocean was still somewhat of a novelty to us, we decided to take a trip with them to a local beach.

While there my mother took this fantastic picture of my father holding the hand of our then fifteen-month-old daughter, Alethea, as she struggled to stand up in the sand with the incoming tide. The intimidating mega-waves, which normally terrified our fledgling little one, seemed to hold no sway over her that day. She just looked around while "Papa Charlie" kept her from falling.

I wish I could say I remember personally seeing the smile on her little face as her Papa Charlie took care of her. In truth, I had nothing to do with that moment.

While my parents watched Alethea down on the shore, Ben and I experienced a very sharp disagreement (to say the least) back in the parking lot. I cannot even remember why we argued. Undoubtedly, the topic of our disparity seemed important to us at the time.

Honestly, it most likely came out of some petty disagreement. I probably would not even remember the argument were it not for that picture reminding me of our whereabouts elsewhere. Realistically, our temperaments that day surely arose out of some deep-seated stress and despair regarding our financial situation, along with other difficulties we experienced at the time.

Our struggles did not come in the form of grand crises or unforgettable tragedy. We did not so much feel broken by any one event. We rather felt sore and weary from the weight of the daily struggle to meet our needs—trying to do so God's way—in that ocean of concrete, temptation, and toil, otherwise known as the city.

In saying this, I do not wish to discredit our many, many positive experiences while there, which greatly outweigh the difficulties. I only mean to say that though life was good, it was also far from easy for us back then. Some days, like that day at the beach, hit us far harder than others.

However, two things that did not worry us at that moment were our toddler's safety or her well-being. The thought of little Ali going anywhere near the shoreline alone or with a stranger would provide us significant cause for alarm. Yet as she stood with my daddy, whom I knew had always kept me safe and healthy, I felt perfectly at ease that he could do the same with her. I had not a shadow of doubt in his ability and desire to greatly care for and love that child whom I love and cherish so greatly.

In fact, at the moment that Mom snapped that picture, Ali's welfare was the furthest thing from my mind. Why would I even need to think about her well-being when I knew she stood in the best possible hands? I imagine that had we focused on what truly mattered to us at the time, namely the safety and well-being of our family, Ben and I would have spent more time enjoying that day rather than battling one another.

I love that picture. I kept it as the wallpaper on my computer for a very long time, and for years I looked at it every chance I got. After several years, it still gives me the greatest feelings of joy and comfort, as if the Lord personally anointed it to breathe peace into my heart at every glance.

GOD'S STORY

Though our situation has improved, I have often carried the same sense of internal storm in my spirit that we felt in California. I have come to realize that I create much of it on my own.

God once addressed these layers of self-made complication with me during a silent retreat. That day I became so aware of the chaos that permeated my soul amidst the external silence that I began to long for a silence that would permeate my soul amidst all external chaos. The Lord offered me such rest through the verses of Psalm 46:

1   God is our refuge and strength,
     an ever-present help in trouble.

2   Therefore we will not fear, though the earth give way
     and the mountains fall into the heart of the sea,

3   though its waters roar and foam
     and the mountains quake with their surging.

4 There is a river whose streams make glad the city of God,
   the holy place where the Most High dwells.

5 God is within her, she will not fall;
   God will help her at break of day.

6 Nations are in uproar, kingdoms fall;
   he lifts his voice, the earth melts.

7 The LORD Almighty is with us;
   the God of Jacob is our fortress.

8 Come and see what the LORD has done,
   the desolations he has brought on the earth.

9 He makes wars cease to the ends of the earth.
   He breaks the bow and shatters the spear;
   he burns the shields with fire.

10 He says, "Be still, and know that I am God;
   I will be exalted among the nations,
   I will be exalted in the earth."

11 The LORD Almighty is with us;
   the God of Jacob is our fortress.

This particular Psalm falls within an eight-chapter series called "The Songs of the Sons of Korah." Korah's family served as church musicians in the days of Kings David and Solomon, some of the first "Praise and Worship" leaders of recorded history.

As with the other Psalms, their honor of God went much deeper than mere thanksgiving for easy times. They sang of the bottomless well of God's goodness amidst distress, injustice, dishonor, and war. They understood that no matter what happened, God maintained control of all things.

They also sang in anticipation of the day when God would make the glory and power of the Lord known to every creature. Knowing that they played for the winning team, they could endure the temporary setbacks of life's various innings. Knowing that God always provides and protects those who trust with obedience, they could meet discomfort and inconvenience with their eyes on the prize.

Or so they sang. Perhaps the Sons of Korah felt exactly as I feel on some days. Perhaps they wrote these songs as both an affirmation and a reminder to themselves, for those days when God seemed particularly far away.

In this "feel good" world where emotions so often rule our choices, these words remind me to focus on that which I know—during those times when the world would otherwise seduce my emotions. Through the Sons of Korah, God offers to weather our storms for us, to allow us to rest fully in grace, and to enter that inner sanctuary that Satan has no authority to touch, much less tear down.

What a beautiful gift! It is hard to imagine a life lived so unreservedly in God's love that literally nothing in this world would have the power to distract me from this holy contentment. Yet God offers this, so freely and fully, to anyone who would but accept it.

I must admit, I usually get in the way of this perfect peace. But there are those small moments of eternity when God's grace overwhelms me to the point where nothing but the Lord matters. Those moments literally come as Heaven on earth.

While I struggle with life's issues, big and small, my loving heavenly Father stands, invisible but not unseen, taking care of everything I hold dear in the midst of life's waves and storms. Given this truth, there is never a real need for anxiety or struggle.

The Fortress keeps me safe from any outside invasion. The mighty Warrior outside the gates breaks all of the enemy's armor. The internal river nurtures and sustains me while the outside war wages. The loving Friend comforts and guides me through it all. So truly, my one and only main concern involves simply staying inside the fort, remaining in God.

One day I happened to be looking at my new favorite picture while thinking about this passage of Scripture. Something therein caused me to weep. That day was not a good day. As a matter of fact, it was one of the worst. As the emotional cocktail of confusion, sadness, fear, and anger flooded my soul, I cried out to God for help.

It then occurred to me how strikingly my father's stance with Ali reflects that nature of my heavenly Daddy whom Psalm 46 describes. I am fortunate to have had a father who has reflected God's nature as both a rock and a fortress, always there when I needed him and ever surrounding me with his arms of love. Both in this picture and throughout my life, "Papa Charlie" pointed me beyond himself to an even greater Daddy, the God who is my eternal fortress.

Then I looked at my daddy's face, and my heavenly Daddy's words, and I instantly knew that everything would be okay. My Daddy, my fortress, would take care of it. At that point I was finally ready to rest in my Lord.

Lord, you are truly all I need. In those moments when my heart surrenders to a holy rest in you, I am truly at peace. I know that you are more than capable of doing all that I cannot, meeting every need that nothing else on this earth can fill. Please crucify all that is in me that keeps me from living out this conviction.

YOUR STORY

Read and reflect upon Psalm 46. Then consider the following questions:

1. Do you know the love of an earthly parent or guardian? If not your own parents, is there a father or mother figure who has guided and helped you feel safe?

2. More importantly, do you know the love of your heavenly Father? If not, I invite you to ask God to show you the Lord's perfect love, and to prepare your heart to receive it.

3. Close your eyes. Make a mental picture of the peaceful river mentioned in the Psalm 46. As you drift on the river within

the fortress of God, imagine yourself floating by and leaving behind all that threatens your safety and well-being. What do you see behind you? What do you see before you?

4. What do you value most in life? Think about what you would give up in order to protect these things. Looking at or thinking of the list of your values, do you believe these values reflect godly priorities? If not, what would it take to get you to change your priorities?

5. Do you trust God to protect the people and things you value most when your values reflect God's will? If so, how do your actions, emotions, and thoughts reflect such a faith? If not, what would it take to get you to trust God to this degree?

6. When was the last time, if ever, that you truly rested in God? What would it take to get you (back) to that point of rest?

7. Read Psalm 46 slowly and return to that first mental picture on the river. Ask the Lord to remove all distraction and doubt, then read it again, out loud this time, and claim each word of the promise for your life. Finally take a few moments of silence to bask in the Lord's providence, and to truly rest in God.

CHAPTER 14

THE BABY'S COMIN'!
Revealed Grace

We know that the whole creation has been groaning as in the pains of childbirth right up to the present time.
Romans 8:22

OUR STORY

Childbirth: it hurts. I mean, it really, really hurts. I've mentioned this before, but the whole intensity of bringing life into the world merits further conversation.

It's also a blessing, one of life's greatest joys. But let's not talk about that part. For a minute, let's imagine what it's like when you strip away the celebration, the anticipation, the bonding, growth, and new life. Let's consider the pain without the promise.

The hurting starts months before the contractions come. First, there is the discomfort of the ever-expanding waistline, and often some sort of incomprehensible combination between increased appetite and morning sickness. And ohhhh the heartburn. Then it gets worse. . . .

Then comes any combination of the following: strange cravings, nausea, heartburn, swelling of so very much of the body, weariness, sleeplessness, fits of anxiety, fits of sadness, fits of giggling, and all kinds of pain or discomfort in parts of the body that you were not previously aware even existed. And let's give a shout-out to all of the loving husbands and family members who do their best to try and meet mama's needs as she tries to appease and accommodate the unborn bundle of joy, and source of anguish, within her womb. This sort of discomfort sometimes subsides a bit later in pregnancy. But the growing needs of the child inside often create more challenges and complications that become a drain on the expectant mother. So yes, it gets worse.

Then come the contractions. Worse? Oh yeah.

For most of us, those moments, and hours, and sometimes days in the delivery room, feel closer to an eternity in length. Those awful contractions seem to last exponentially longer than the seconds used up on the ticking clock. And all too often, just when you think you can't take it anymore . . . it gets worse . . . so much worse.

On a certain level, even the expectant father can relate to the anguish to some degree. In addition to the sympathy pains that come from seeing the woman you love most in anguish while in delivery, many of you gentlemen are brave enough to hold your ladies' hands during contractions. And I don't know about the rest of you ladies, but the more I hurt when delivering our daughter, the harder I squeezed Ben's hand, and I went for his fingers. I honestly think I almost broke them, or at least bruised the bones.

Likewise, adoptive parents experience a different kind of "labor" pain. They often must make great financial sacrifices, experience grueling adoption processes, and wait for an undetermined amount of time, often up to years, for their child to come.

When isolated from the context of joy and blessing that childbirth offers, the labor itself feels like death.

But the context of new life gives the labor pains a purpose. Not only does this make the seemingly unbearable more doable, but the overall experience and results are enough to compel countless women to actively choose and seek this excruciating pain over and over again. In some strange way, the pain and struggle ultimately even serve to enhance the joy that comes when the child is born.

When you think about it, almost nothing enduring and worth having comes completely free of labor pains. Any truly and deeply joyful person I know had to go through something pretty intense to get to that depth of fulfillment in their life. Still, the feeling while in the moment of anguish is no fun at all.

MY STORY

This book was almost 15 years in the making. Toward the beginning, I wrote these introductory words: "I believe that God can grant any of us victory and peace right within the struggle, while at the same time constantly moving us forward in grace." Over the past decade and a half, God has written and rewritten that truth in my heart. It was as if the Lord inspired those words as a prophecy to myself, with which came the promise that the Lord would prove them over and over again.

I finished the first draft (about half the length of the final product) almost immediately, grateful for all the life lessons God had taught me, and for the opportunity to share about God's grace with others. Little did I know that God had more in store for this book, and my life. And let me tell you, it was a difficult birth. In the beginning it felt like the issues with our house and the renter were about the worst things I could ever endure. But that was only the beginning of the labor pains.

I originally drafted chapter 13 as an article to be published in the Father's Day edition of a magazine. That was one of the last things that Daddy could read and understand. Within a year of when Mom took the picture I mentioned of my father with my daughter on the beach, he was diagnosed with dementia. He soon showed specific signs of Alzheimer's disease. For the following decade I felt powerless as I watched Daddy's mind, and eventually his body, slip away little by little.

I am so grateful for the godly example of my mother, who embodied *agape* (unconditional), *phileo* (companion/friend), and *eros* (romantic) love at their very best throughout the whole process. Nevertheless, watching one of the two men you love most in this world, your hero, escape from your earthly grasp, is not easy. What a bittersweet struggle to have to slowly, little by little, release my earthly papa into the arms of my heavenly one. Yet I know that even this slow death was a form of labor pain into greater things. To use the words of a famous prayer for peace, "It is in dying that we are born to eternal life.[5]"

Even as Daddy's body broke, so much of our own life seemed to deteriorate, and not even our best efforts seemed to make it better. To be honest, these past few years have been marked by constant, intense struggle in one form or another.

Here are some highlights:

- Car trouble—After spending all of our money on "reliable" transportation, we had four different cars in a row die on us in one year. During this period, three different friends had car issues with the vehicles they had loaned us, while we were using them. This makes matters near impossible when living in a small farm town of less than five hundred people, an eight-mile drive from the nearest grocery store.

- Unexpected medical bills—One year began with an emergency appendectomy, got filled with thousands of dollars of medical bills, and ended with Ben being attacked by a stray cat, which cost more than all of the other bills combined. This happened while I was unemployed, the house was falling apart, and health insurance through Ben's work cost us over a fourth of Ben's income. At the time Ben made eighteen dollars too much a month for us to receive any financial help whatsoever with medical bills.

- Zero income—At one point, we went three full months without any income other than $180 in food stamps per month. At other points, we would go a few weeks or a month without income or were living on as little as $75 per week. In retrospect, this is a

---

5 This prayer was written anonymously and attributed to St. Francis, though it was not found among any of his writings. The earliest form of this prayer dates back to 1912, and it was in French. (St. Francis lived in the middle ages and was Italian.)

great, great testimony as to how God provided even in the direst circumstances.

- Financial ruin—The recession hit hard. Without ever being fired, my husband and I lost a combined fifteen jobs over about a decade. Combined with car issues, extremely expensive house repairs, and all of the necessary moves it took to chase whatever job would pay our bills, this depleted all of our financial reserves and left us tens of thousands of dollars in debt until we finally had no credit left, no more resources, and no options. At one point we were within days of homelessness and ended up living in our friend's one-bedroom summer camper for about four months.

- Always on the move—We tried to stay in town for about two and a half years after my first lay-off, but the jobs just weren't there. Then came all of the moves to chase the jobs that never seemed to work out. We lived in six different cities across three different states over a period of just over four years. Between the beginning of first and the end of sixth grade, Alethea attended seven different schools. We had never wanted this much change, but we had to eat.

- Loss of loved ones—While God has always provided an abundance of phenomenal friends and support networks for our family, we spent years marked by some intense periods of death, loss, and betrayal. Some close friends and dear causes in which we had invested wounded us deeply. We have said far too many tearful goodbyes to great people when we moved away to try and chase gainful employment. Our own marital relationship has been maximumly strained, and perhaps even broken a time or two. One year we said a final goodbye to eight close friends and family members who passed away in an eleven-month period. One of the most difficult goodbyes came when our beautiful ten-year-old niece fell into Jesus's arms less than a year after being diagnosed with an incurable brain cancer. In the midst of this we even lost our beloved dog, Spot, the one consistent thing we got to bring with us, as he was struck by clear blue lightning at the start of an anomalous September hailstorm.

- No sleep, no family, no support—Ben worked one particularly abusive job that moved his hours and shifts so much that he literally went about two full years without a single decent night's sleep. He spent three full months in a row living on no more than ten hours a week of sleep. He often went without any sleep at all. Because of our opposing schedules, we had little time to spend as a family. The time we did have together was often spent doing things for the church at which I worked at the time. In the meantime, his workplace was not only non-Christian, it was anti-Christian. Some of his fellow employees were literally witches from the local spiritist community who spoke incantations, curses, and spells against him. This sounds spooky and unreal, but the reality, in the words of Paul, is that "Many live as enemies of the cross of Christ" (Philippians 3:18). This set the stage for the most difficult, most painful labor pains of my entire life.

Then it got worse, so much worse.
Then came the total breakdown.
Over a decade of constant crisis, deprivation, struggle, and ever-worsening conditions, combined with the extreme conditions in his work environment, finally broke my husband. And that broke me.

Within a month of preaching a sermon on total surrender to God, and beginning preliminary applications for us both to go into full-time ordained ministry, Ben made a sudden, direct turn the other way. My godly, warrior husband who had tried for so long to serve God and meet our families' needs suddenly and decisively decided to go in the exact opposite direction.

On the day after our thirteenth anniversary, and just a few days after my being laid off, Ben declared to me that he had married the wrong woman. This announcement came while we were in the middle of the process of candidacy for ordination as full-time pastors. Just two months after we were declared a healthy, committed marriage by a family psychologist who had evaluated us as part of the process.

I asked about all the convictions and declarations he had made about loving me and living for God and our family, about all the sermons and Bible lessons he had taught. Ben said that he realized he had just had it all wrong, that he had been confused. His level of true confusion in that moment was nothing less than demonic. This was not the man I had married, or even the man I had known two months before.

I had just finished a term of paid lay ministry within my church that came with house, phone, and a laptop. I was allowed to keep all three as long as the two of us were pursuing ordained ministry together. Ben's turn for the worse also dictated my own withdrawal from the process, at least temporarily, and thus negated my access to all three resources. Since our personal car was in Ben's name, and he needed a way to work, he kept it.

The pastors were understanding, kind, and patient with me, and they did not make me leave immediately. But I needed to make arrangements for moving, living, and caring for our daughter within just a few weeks, having little to no resources to do so. So in a very real sense, I lost my phone, my computer, my car, my home, my husband, my job, and all of my plans for the future all within a few days. I don't know how I would have made it were it not for the extreme generosity of good friends who allowed us to stay in their small guest cottage, for a year and a half, refusing to ever take payment for their extreme hospitality during our time of need.

During that dark period there were days when I could do nothing but cry out, literally scream out, at God in pain and anguish. Sometimes it physically hurt to breathe. During that time, I learned to seek out the promises of God's Word like never before, and to cling to them for dear life. They were all I had, and in truth, they were all I needed.

I heard God saying to me that I should work on myself and trust God to work on Ben. I sensed that the best way to fight for my husband, my marriage, and my life was on my knees. That was so much harder than it sounded because I really like to be the boss, and I really wanted to take charge of my healing. But all illusion of control had been stripped from me. That was unimaginably painful, but it was a useful birthing pain.

The only sense of power I felt at that time was grounded in the foundation of God's Word. I read, reread, and claimed the promises about joy, restoration, healing, and my authority as God's child to persistently pray with boldness for God to grant my request according to God's will. I felt so weak. I was so weak. But God was and always is so very strong.

Through the labor pains I learned that I need not feel the blessings and provision of God at every point in order to believe and claim them. In fact, it shatters the powers of darkness in unspeakable ways when we choose to persist as warriors praising and worshipping God even when our emotions and circumstances beg us to retreat. At many moments of that "dark night of the soul," as some would call it, I would hear God quietly say to me, "Will you still praise me?" My spirit was just stubborn enough to take that as a challenge not to quit.

Sometimes it takes a total break to lead to complete healing and restoration. It would take another book to explain all that followed over the next few years. In a nutshell, Ben came back, fairly quickly, and God slowly renovated our whole lives in a way that made us better than new.

I will say we have come out of the past fifteen years better and more healed, both as individuals and as a married couple, than when we started. The difficulties brought to light some deep wounds that had been festering under the surface of our faith for years, wounds that only God could heal. It also rechartered our life's course from a path that seemed right to us at the time. Where we were going was not immoral or bad, but God had better plans for us.

Because the punctures were deep, the healing has been deep. And I can tell you that my marriage is better today than it has ever been. We still face trials and disagreements, but I am married to a hard-working man of integrity who loves God and his family with everything in him.

I had no idea how many people face the same issues that plagued my family until we went through them ourselves. We have been able to help others simply because we have been through what they are now facing. Helping them is part of our own continual healing, because in reminding others about God's grace in our life, we also remind ourselves. I find that I need those reminders.

And today I tell you with conviction, I wouldn't trade the trials, not a single one. I wouldn't even trade the mistakes, because I serve the great recycler. As the expert artisan, our Lord can work every shade of our lives—no matter how broken, bruised, or bloody they seem to us—into a great masterpiece for God's glory and our good. And I refuse to give back those amazing fruits that God has grown within my life through that soil of adversity.

I have come to realize that what once felt like death has really been labor pains for the greater things to come.

GOD'S STORY

As far as kingship was concerned, David was the whole package: a gifted statesman, an accomplished musician, a successful warrior, a loyal friend, and a drop-dead gorgeous hottie. Most importantly, he was described as a man after God's own heart. Even as God revealed to him that his royal line would be established forever, his response was to bow in humility and praise the Lord.

David was not without his shortcomings and mistakes, for which he paid dearly throughout his lifetime. Yet in the end he always seemed to come back to his faith in and reliance upon the Lord. The combination of his wisdom, gifts, and fiercely loyal warrior servants laid the foundation for the greatest period of peace and prosperity in Israel's history.

David was also a caveman.[6] And by that, I mean that for a period of time he literally lived in a cave. His many early accomplishments had earned him the role of personal musician to King Saul, then commander of Saul's army, and eventually the king's son-in-law. Some of those same gifts eventually led Saul to see him as a threat and make several attempts on his life. David could not at the time seek solace from the neighboring kings, whose armies he had defeated. Instead, "David . . . escaped to the cave of Adullam" (1 Samuel 22:1).

This was not the only cave where David stayed. With Saul in hot pursuit, he could not stay in one place for long. Instead, he moved throughout the wilderness, laying his head wherever he could find rest and cover from Saul and his army. This cat and mouse chase continued for over ten years.

Even while David wore King Saul's label as "felon at large," people seemed to be drawn to him. As an outlaw, however, David drew a different kind of a crowd: "All those who were in distress or in debt or discontented gathered around him, and he became their commander. About four hundred men were with him" (1 Samuel 22:2).

This number continued to increase throughout David's wilderness escape route. So basically, David went from being the commander of the "winners" (Saul's powerful army) to being the lord of the misfits, the king of the cavemen. It is not so much that these men and their families were unfit citizens or warriors. Yet they seemed to identify themselves as outcasts, forgotten and tossed aside by society. They were not unvaluable, but they had been devalued.

The book of 1 Chronicles tells several tales of the great heroes and warriors in the time of King David. These mighty men as the Bible calls them, were the people who had joined David as outcasts and misfits during his time of hiding from Saul in the wilderness. The most influential people in helping build the great kingdom of Israel

---

6 Both the images of God birthing new things in my life and the value of time spent proverbially "in the cave," as David did, came from various sermons and talks by Pastor Timothy P. Smart of REALiFE Church.

were the same ones who years before had felt ignored at best, rejected at worst by this very nation that they eventually helped lead. And their leader, King David, once again ruled over the very army who had once sought his life.

There was a fifteen-to-twenty-year gap between the time the prophet Samuel secretly anointed David as king over Israel and when he actually took the throne. Some might argue that David's time in service to Saul and in command over Saul's army well prepared him for kingship. While this would have made some contribution to his preparation, I believe there were other more important factors involved.

It took the cave to make the king. It took the labor and struggle to birth the man after God's heart, the seed whose offspring would both embody and fulfill God's eternal promise.

It took the cave to make the warriors, David's mightiest men, with unwavering loyalty that was birthed in their shared hardship and struggle.

It took the hard labor to birth the greatness in God's people.

In my birthing class, the term "pain with a purpose" came up over and over again. I heard the message loud and clear: it wasn't going to be easy, but it would all be worth it in the end. So, I could actually count the suffering as cause for joy and hopeful anticipation.

Childbirth labor is the most acute example of so much of life. According to God's Word, absolutely everything works out for the good of those who love the Lord (Romans 8:28). So, in effect, when we love and serve God with everything we have, any suffering and difficulty is pain with a purpose. This life serves as a birthing room for the eternal.

Whatever our situation or station in life, God wants to birth something new and beautiful in us all. We are all welcomed into the victorious arms of a loving Father, the winning team, to live according to God's persistent promise for greater things in us. When we see the fruits before us, praise God for favor and promises fulfilled. During the trials and challenges, we can lean into our hope, our confident expectation that God will work it all for our good, and that it will be worth the wait.

When true hope is deferred, it is gaining interest. So, don't cash it in for something far less profitable. To give up our confident expectation in the one true God and God's promises in exchange for *anything* this world has to offer is like prematurely cashing in a ten-million-dollar savings bond for a few weeks' pay.

If you are trying to be faithful but you're stuck in the pain, keep pressing into God's promise, because the baby's comin'! When you look for and claim God's favor, you will see more of it in this life. And praise the Lord. No matter what our station in life, those of us who have placed our faith in Christ *always* have a hope both within and beyond this life's sufferings. We are victorious, blessed, and beloved, and it is only a matter of time before even Satan's lies of defeat (the only real power he has) will be completely crushed.

I wonder how our lives might differ if we actually believed that and practice it in every iota of our lives.

I'm still in labor. I'm still a mess. We all are. And God is still God.

I am God's sloppy, beautiful, flawed, perfect, struggling, victorious, weak, conquering, limited, gifted, audacious, loving, frustrated, calm, sometimes discouraged, but always anointed, mess. And I wouldn't have it any other way.

How about you?

Every other chapter in this book has included a prayer by the author. For this final chapter, take some time to write your own prayer to God. Think of the end of this book as the beginning of a new volume in your own story of faith.

YOUR STORY

Read and reflect upon Romans 8:18–39. Then consider the following questions:

1. Explain the comparison Romans 8:22 makes between our present life and labor pains. How are the two alike?

2. Think about a time when God allowed you to go through something extremely painful in order to birth something new in you. How did you feel and think about it at the time? How do you feel and think about it now?

3. Verse 25 talks about hope. The original Greek word used for hope in this passage, *elpis*, means confident expectation. Think of it in terms of a child waiting for Christmas. What gifts are you looking forward to receiving when you meet Jesus face to face? What gifts do you look forward to receiving while here on earth? How might the definition of hope as confident expectation (rather than uncertain wishing) change our attitude toward God?

4. Consider verse 28 in terms of God as the great recycler, one who can redeem the filthiest, trashiest, and most worthless of circumstances by using them to bring about great beauty and worth. Is there anything or anyone you know that seems unredeemable? Is there anything in your own life or heart that you consider unredeemable? Take a moment and listen for God to bring the truth to light in your heart. Consider laying this person, this thing, or this aspect of your life at God's feet and confessing your confidence that God can work even this, especially this, to God's glory and your good. Remember, confession is all about declaring God's truth, even when you don't feel it.

5. Verses 35–39 talk about God's undefeatable love that will stick to us throughout everything. It also describes those who love Christ as "more than conquerors." What role does God's love play in our victories, both in and beyond this life?

6. I Samuel tells the story of David's life before he became king. Consider the struggles of David and his men as they moved around from place to place and even lived in caves. How do you think these experiences might have prepared them to eventually lead and protect the kingdom of Israel? Have you ever felt like one of these cavemen—outcast, misunderstood, and powerless when you were just trying to do the right thing? How did God use this time in your life? If you are in that struggle right now, how might God use this in your life?

7. To anoint people or things literally means to pour oil upon them as a way to show that they are set apart for a special purpose. What does the word *anointed* mean to you for your own life? Do you believe that God has anointed you? How does God use you to bring blessing and show God's love to others? How does God bless you as you seek to do this?

ORDER INFORMATION

To order additional copies of this book, please visit
www.redemption-press.com.
Also available on Amazon.com and BarnesandNoble.com
Or by calling toll free 1-844-2REDEEM.

CPSIA information can be obtained
at www.ICGtesting.com
Printed in the USA
JSHW020108240621
16205JS00003B/206